HARRY HAFT

Religion, Theology, and the Holocaust
Steven T. Katz, *Series Editor*

HARRY (HERSCHEL) HAFT
Fast Rising Light Heavyweight Contender·
Mgr:· Harry Brooks Mandell-3155 Bedford Ave.Bklyn.·, N.Y.
Phone-Navarre 8-3593-Col. 5-8700.

Harry Haft, professional prizefighter.
Courtesy of Alan Haft.

HARRY HAFT

Auschwitz Survivor, Challenger of Rocky Marciano

ALAN SCOTT HAFT

With Forewords by John Radzilowski and Mike Silver

SYRACUSE UNIVERSITY PRESS

First Paperback Edition 2020

20   21   22   23   24   25   6   5   4   3   2   1

∞ The paper used in this publication meets the minimum requirements
of the American National Standard for Information Sciences—Permanence of Paper for
Printed Library Materials, ANSI Z39.48–1992.

For a listing of books published and distributed by Syracuse University Press,
visit https://press.syr.edu.

ISBN: 978-0-8156-1119-6 (paperback)
978-0-8156-0823-3 (hardcover)
978-0-8156-0800-4 (e-book)

Library of Congress cataloged the hardcover as follows:

Haft, Alan Scott.
Harry Haft : Auschwitz survivor, challenger of Rocky Marciano / Alan Scott Haft ; with
Forewords by John Radzilowski and Mike Silver.— 1st ed.
p. cm.—(Religion, theology, and the Holocaust)
ISBN 0–8156–0823–3 (hardcover : alk. paper)
1. Haft, Harry, 1925– 2. Jews—Poland—Belchatów—Biography. 3. Holocaust survivors—
United States—Biography. 4. Jewish boxers—United States—Biography. I. Title. II. Series.
DS135.P63H334734 2006
796.83092—dc22
2006001870

To my father

"After all I've been through, what harm can
a man with gloves on his hands do to me?"

—Harry Haft, 1948

ALAN SCOTT HAFT is a 1973 graduate of Queens College in New York. He received his J.D. from the University of Miami Law School in 1978. He currently lives in Albuquerque, New Mexico, with his wife, Gail. They have two children, Hartley and Jamie.

Contents

PART TWO: DREAMS

Illustrations

Foreword

Jewish Life in Poland

JOHN RADZILOWSKI

THE HASIDIC JEWS of east-central Poland explain their rich tradition of storytelling with a story. There was once a wise and holy rebbe who was known far and wide as the leader of his community to whom problems of the gravest sort should be referred. When hardships and danger faced his community, all eyes would turn to the rebbe. When peril threatened the people, the rebbe would go to a secret place in the forest, light a special fire, and say a special prayer. When he did this, God would hear and the peril would pass. His successor was also a very learned rebbe. When hard times threatened the community, he, too, would go out to the special place in the forest. However, as a young man he had never learned to light the special fire. So he would merely say the special prayer and it was enough. God would listen and the hardships would pass. The successor of this rebbe was also a very holy and respected man, but he never learned how to find that special place in the forest. So when danger threatened the community he would stay home and say the special prayer, and it was enough. God would listen and the community would be spared. Now his successor was also a great rebbe, but he had forgotten how to say the special prayer. So when hard times came to his people he would go to his study and shut the door and sit at his desk. "Oh God," he would pray, "I don't know how to make the special fire and I cannot find the place in the forest, and I have forgotten how to say the prayer, but I can tell you the story." And this was enough. God listened and the hard times would end. The moral is that God made man because he loves a good story.

The life of Harry Haft is one of those stories. Like so many memoirs of Holocaust survivors, it is a story of survival, of the strange tricks of fate that leave one person alive and another dead. It is about an encounter with evil in its most extreme form. It is about what happens after the immediate danger is past when a man must put the shards of his life back together and somehow make sense of it all while in the shadow of terrible memories that never fade far enough into oblivion. Yet, Haft's story is also different. He is not an unambiguous hero who stands aloof from the madness of the camps, as so many memoirists portray themselves.

Harry Haft grew up in the town of Belchatow, near the industrial city of Lodz. Like Lodz, Belchatow grew thanks to its textile mills. Founded as a village in 1391, by 1820 the town had a population of only about three hundred, one-third of whom were Jewish. Following the Napoleonic wars and Poland's loss of independence to Germany, Austria, and Russia, Belchatow fell under Russian domination. The area received significant investment and became a center for cloth-making, especially to supply the Russian market. As the town's textile industry grew, Belchatow drew many Jews from the surrounding regions who came to work in the mills. By 1860, its population had reached nearly 1,500.

More than three quarters of the population was Jewish. During the January Uprising against Russian rule in 1863–64, the town supported the insurgents and was punished with a revocation of its status and by punitive tariffs that made selling its cloth in Russia much more difficult. World War I brought more misery as the German army occupied the region and systematically looted the inhabitants. As the war dragged on, the region's factories were cannibalized for spare parts to keep mills in Germany running. After the war, Poland regained its independence and the textile industry began to revive and Belchatow's population began to grow once more, this time drawing in Polish peasants to work in the textile mills. Although a significant number of Jews continued to labor in the mills, many also worked as craftsmen and small merchants, supplying the town's growing population with goods and services.

In the 1920s, the developments in Belchatow were part of a larger effort of a newly independent Poland to put itself back together again after years of war and 123 years of foreign rule. After the war, basic infrastructure was a shambles. So many farms had been looted or destroyed that the country could not feed itself. Although American food aid administered by future U.S. President Herbert Hoover saved millions from starvation, malnutrition was one of the leading causes of death, especially among children and the elderly. Diseases such as typhoid and cholera reached epidemic proportions. Banditry and lawlessness were common in many parts of the country as authorities struggled to provide basic services.

Structural problems were even more serious and almost every facet of public life had to be rebuilt from scratch. The economic legacy of the Partitions meant that each zone was oriented toward markets that either no longer existed or were closed to Polish exports. The textile factories of Lodz and Belchatow had once produced cloth for the Russian marketplace. The farmers of western Poland had shipped their produce to Berlin and the German mar-

ket. Both of these markets were now gone. Several different cur-
rencies were in circulation from the three partitioning powers and
money printed for the occupation zones. All of these had to be re-
called and reorganized. Three different legal systems were in
place. The Russian partition even used a different rail gauge so all
the railroad lines had to be converted to standard gauge.

Since in the Russian and German zones of partitioned Poland,
Poles had been kept out of most administrative positions, the only
cadre of experienced civil servants was found in Austrian Galicia.
So the only officials with a modicum of administrative experience
were those whose outlook was shaped by the sclerotic Austrian
bureaucracy, whose major contribution to civilization had been to
inspire the work of Czech author Franz Kafka.

Poland also struggled to develop a democratic government.
The country had a long tradition of parliamentary rule and had
created only the world's second democratic constitution, based on
the American example. Nevertheless, party, regional, and ethnic
divisions and years of living under the rule of autocratic regimes
left the Polish political scene deeply divided. After independence,
weak governments rose and fell in rapid succession. In 1926, Marshal Josef Pilsudski, who led Poland to victory over a massive Soviet invasion in 1920, staged a coup. Pilsudski's goal was to create
a stable government, which he succeeded in doing for time. The
price, however, was a suspension of the normal democratic
processes that retarded the development of a new cadre of political leaders. After 1926, Poland had a form of mild authoritarism in
which the pro-government parties controlled the national government and those who opposed Pilsudski were consigned to perma-
nent opposition. There was no serious effort to curtail most civil
liberties such as freedom of the press, though mass demonstra-

tions by the peasants and the right-wing opposition were often met with a fierce police response. (The major exception to this was the repression of the nationalist movement among the Ukrainian minority in southeastern Poland.)

Under Pilsudski, Poland had a reasonably strong and modern military. Until the Depression, its economy grew. The country also rebuilt its infrastructure, expanded basic literacy, improved public health, stabilized its currency, and created a functioning governmental system. In foreign policy, Poland remained allied to France. During Hitler's rise to power in Germany in 1933, Pilsudski even proposed a joint Polish-French invasion to remove the new Nazi leader, a suggestion that was flatly rejected in Paris as mad warmongering. As France and Britain stood aside and let Germany rearm, the Poles sought to keep both Germany and Stalin's Soviet Union at arm's length.

Pilsudski died in May 1935. His successors, the so-called Regime of the Colonels, were weak men without the stature of the old marshal. As Pilsudski had been purely pragmatic, he had left no guidelines for his successors to follow, leaving them to guess what he would have done. To shore up political support, the government attempted to appeal to anti-Semitic sentiments that were common among the rightist opposition, especially the National Democratic Party, led by Roman Dmowski, which was the largest single party in Poland, with about 30 percent of the electorate. Pilsudski had been philo-Semitic and had had Jewish comrades in arms from his earliest days as an underground anti-Russian conspirator. The largest Jewish party, the conservative Agudat Israel, supported Pilsudski's pro-government bloc.

After Pilsudski's death, the government attempted to enact a ban on ritual slaughter and turned an increasingly blind eye to discrimination against Jews in government service and education. The new leadership's anti-Semitic moves, however, failed to bring any additional support. Rhetoric aside, its actions were never enough to attract the Polish right, which had fundamental conflicts with the government and not merely over policy toward Jews. Yet, the anti-Semitic tone drove away Jewish parties and a large segment of the Polish Socialist Party. In 1938, the results of local and municipal elections were a clear defeat for the government while the growing crisis with Nazi Germany made anti-Semitism increasingly unpopular. Although the period of "official" anti-Semitism had been brief, it had done significant damage to Polish-Jewish relations.

Jewish life in Poland during the years of Harry Haft's youth was a picture of great achievement tempered by internal and external conflict. By 1939, over 3.3 million Jews lived in Poland, constituting 10 percent of the population. This percentage was much higher in cities, especially in eastern Poland. Warsaw had the largest Jewish community, with 40 percent of the city being Jewish. Pinsk, in the eastern marches, was 80 percent Jewish. Significant numbers of Jews also resided in rural towns and villages. The shtetls in these communities ranged from a few hundred inhabitants to a few thousand. Some were prosperous and supported a variety of community institutions, others too poor or too small to even support a synagogue.

Although Zionism and socialism had made significant inroads, the majority of Jews remained traditional and culturally conservative. While Hebrew was increasingly common among the Jewish elite, Yiddish was still the primary language of everyday life. Although most Jews knew at least some Polish, the majority did not speak it well and some did not speak it at all. About a tenth of the Jewish population, however, was highly assimilated into the Polish mainstream, preferred to speak Polish, and were well represented in the Polish cultural, academic, and professional elite. Jews made up nearly half of the country's doctors and lawyers.

Jews could be found in every socioeconomic category from the richest to the poorest. On average, Jews were slightly better off than Poles, Belarusians, and Ukrainians, the majority of whom remained peasant farmers. Most Jews were small merchants or craftsmen, but this ran the gamut from prosperous store owners to peddlers and tinkers who eked out a living selling small items to peasants.

Jewish cultural life flourished. There were about thirty daily newspapers and more than 130 Jewish periodicals in circulation before the outbreak of war in 1939, not counting many smaller local publications. Assimilated Polish Jews made major contributions to a shared Polish and Jewish literature. Aphorist Stanislaw Jerzy Lec; Julian Tuwim, the leader of the Skamander group of experimental poets; and the brilliant writer and illustrator Bruno Schulz were well known and highly regarded among both the Jewish and Christian intellectual elite. Author and children's welfare expert Janusz Korczak pioneered new ideas of childcare. He was also the author of *King Matt the First*, one of the most widely read children's books in prewar Poland. Yiddish-language theater, music, and film were widespread, forming a large "niche" market.

The great problem of prewar Jewish life could be found in the contradictory impulses of wanting to be included in mainstream Polish society and yet wishing to remain wholly separate. Polish Christian society—itself deeply divided on the place and role of minorities—experienced similar contradictions of wishing for assimilation and seeking to keep Jews at arm's length. Economic hardships, especially brought on by the Depression, heightened tensions and increased anti-Semitism. Polish nationalists attempted to stage periodic local boycotts of Jewish-owned businesses and campaigns to "buy Polish." All of these efforts failed and much of the local trade, particularly in eastern Poland, remained in Jewish hands. Yet the threat of boycotts and the generally poor economic conditions ensured that Jewish small business struggled to survive.

Education was another flashpoint, and groups of Jewish and Christian students had frequent scuffles that sometimes resulted in more serious violence. In 1930, Jewish students in Wilno killed a nationalist student, sparking an anti-Jewish riot. With space in universities limited, in the 1930s some nationalists made efforts to place quotas on Jewish students and to restrict Jews who did get in to special "ghetto benches" in the back of the classroom. At schools where such measures were implemented, Jewish students refused to sit and were joined by sympathetic Polish students in standing throughout the lectures.

Feelings of antagonism went both ways, as some Jews felt nothing but contempt for Poles and the notion of going to Palestine to build a possible future Jewish state grew more attractive. At the same time, there were numerous examples of good relations and friendships that went across ethnic and religious lines. Politics also made for alliances. The Jewish Bund worked with the PPS. The right-wing Zionist Revisionists trained with the Polish army and joined with nationalist paramilitary groups in battling left-wing opponents. The majority of Poles and Jews, however, remained indifferent to one another, interacting only in limited circumstances. This arrangement was not so much a result of antagonism but of a profound sense of difference. Each community lived in a self-contained world of its own and rarely needed to interact with the other.

Yet, for all the problems, the situation of Jews in Poland was by no means the worst in Europe and was clearly superior to that in most neighboring countries. It is possible that over time, Poles and Jews would have worked out better mutual relations, muddling through good times and bad side by side. Both communities, and the country as a whole, lacked leaders of vision who could have changed the situation. Tragically, neither Poles nor Jews would have the time to resolve their differences.

On September 1, 1939, Adolf Hitler's armies attacked Poland, soon joined by the armies of Hitler's Soviet ally, beginning the fourth and most terrible partition of Poland. The Nazi conquest dramatically increased the number of Jews living under German control, but early in war there was no clear policy on what to do with the Jews, let alone other "subhuman" groups such as Poles or Gypsies. Early Nazi policy in Poland was designed to murder the Polish leadership—politicians, businessmen, professors, teachers, doctors, clergy, lawyers, and nobility—and to terrorize and segregate the Jewish community. Western areas of Poland were to be "Germanized" and incorporated into the Reich. Central Poland, including the area of Belchatow, was part of the German occupation zone—the General Government. Although mass extermination was not yet a reality, early German policies—including mass deportations, mobile killing squads, and segregation by ethnicity—pointed the way to the Final Solution.

Towns like Belchatow were designed to have ghettos, a Nazi vehicle for ethnic segregation and as collection points for the populations of smaller Jewish communities from surrounding areas who were gradually concentrated in regional centers. To begin with, few ghettos had walls or were actively guarded by German troops. German resources and organization had not yet reached a level that would allow for such complete segregation. Instead, the Nazis attempted a form of self-policing using separate Jewish and Polish police forces and fostering a sense of antagonism between the communities. Nevertheless, old patterns of behavior proved hard to break. Poles and Jews continued to do business with one another, and tough, enterprising young men like Harry Haft could make a decent living working the black market. Local Polish and Jewish police were often willing to look the other way for a little money, food, or liquor.

It rarely occurred to Jews that they should flee the "open" ghettos—there was no way to predict the future. A few guessed what might be coming, but these were mainly people who spoke good Polish and had close personal or professional ties to gentiles who could provide the necessary support network to help them survive and "pass" as Christians. Most Jews had no such connections, and it simply did not occur to them to leave their homes and families and take a chance among people they considered alien. As German rule grew ever more repressive, the ghettos were gradually sealed.

In 1941, Hitler turned on his ally Stalin and German armies attacked the USSR. Then, the huge Jewish populations of eastern Poland came under Nazi control and the immediate response was the use of Einsatzgruppen, or mobile killing squads. Pioneered during the German invasion of Poland in 1939, the Einsatzgruppen systematically massacred the inhabitants of the Jewish shtetls of Belarus, Ukraine, and Lithuania. In the midst of this horrible carnage, German commanders became concerned over the psychological damage to their own men from killing women and children. As a result, German leaders sought a more "humane" way of murdering Jews and other undesirables. This impulse to shield their own people from the full horror of their own policies would result in the development of gas chambers and crematoria. Thus was born the Final Solution, carried out in death camps like Treblinka and Auschwitz-Birkenau.

The Nazis had developed concentration camps early in their reign in Germany to house political enemies. In 1939, this system was extended to occupied Poland. The infamous camp at Auschwitz was created in 1940 to hold Polish political prisoners, though its functions soon expanded to include other nationalities and ultimately the killing of Jews. In addition to imprisoning potential opponents of the Nazi regime, the camps also served as a kind of business enterprise. The German government and private businesses exploited the labor of prisoners to make products for the war or to sell on the open market.

Beginning in 1942, the Germans also began to set up camps with the sole purpose of killing Jews—most notoriously Treblinka and Majdanek. These were located near major Jewish population centers and close to railroad lines that would facilitate the rapid transfer of Jews from ghettos to killing sites. Auschwitz existed both as a camp for political prisoners and slave laborers as well as a killing center. In addition to gassing, prisoners were killed by overwork, starvation, execution, torture, and disease. By the end of the war, this ruthless, industrialized approach to mass murder resulted in the deaths of about three million Polish Jews, as well as three million Jews from the rest of Europe. In addition, the Nazis exterminated some two million Polish gentiles and some 750,000 Roma, or Gypsies.

As the Germans began to "liquidate" ghettos, many Jews

sought to flee the extermination. The local gentile population, caught up in its own troubles, had little time to spare for Jews. In some cases, Poles helped themselves to Jewish property. Gangs of blackmailers made up of both Poles and Jews, though small in number, did terrible damage to Jews in hiding. The Gestapo had deadly units of "Jew catchers" who specialized in trapping Jews in hiding.

Nevertheless, large numbers of Jews found hiding places among the Poles despite the risk of death for both fugitives and rescuers. In Warsaw, for example, an estimated 28,000 Jews lived in hiding after the liquidation of the ghetto. Though it took only one person to betray a fugitive, it took a network of about twenty-five people to hide a single Jew. Polish resistance activist Irena Sendler personally saved the lives of some two thousand Jewish children. Captured by the Gestapo and brutally tortured, Sendler refused to betray her charges. Although Sendler miraculously survived, most captured rescuers and the Jews they assisted were not so lucky, and many thousands would die before firing squads or in the gas chambers.

In the end, there was little either Poles or Jews could do in the face of overwhelming German military power. Only the complete destruction of the Third Reich would stop the Holocaust, though historians continue to debate whether Allied military planners could have taken action to slow the Nazis' machinery of death.

Nevertheless, as Haft's story shows, the Nazis failed. They failed to destroy the Jewish people. They failed to crush the spirit of resistance and the human will to survive and live in freedom. Though many survivors such as Haft had to bear a terrible burden in the years after liberation, their struggle to live despite the worst horrors humanity could dream up for itself remains among the greatest stories in human history.

Foreword

New York City, the Mob, and the Prizefighter Harry Haft, 1948–1949

MIKE SILVER

WHEN HARRY HAFT ARRIVED in New York City in the spring of 1948, America was in the midst of a postwar economic boom. The twenty-two-year-old Holocaust survivor could have easily secured a low-paying, menial job. Instead, he chose a path already well trod in years past by thousands of other poor immigrants, or their sons.

Harry Haft became a professional prizefighter.

Today most people are unaware that during the first half of the twentieth century, professional boxing was a major spectator sport in America, rivaling baseball in popularity. Even fewer people are aware that Jews were active in the sport in great numbers both as boxers and in supporting roles that included managers, trainers, promoters, equipment manufacturers, and publishers (boxing magazines and books).

Jewish athletes were so prolific in boxing that by the late 1920s almost one-third of all professional fighters in America were Jewish. Between 1900 and 1939, twenty-four Jewish American boxers won world championships. Great fighters such as New York's

Benny Leonard, Chicago's Barney Ross, and Philadelphia's Lew Tendler became folk heroes in Jewish neighborhoods and, for many, powerful symbols of ethnic pride and achievement.

At a time when boxing mattered to society far more than it does today Jewish prizefighters were major players. Their contribution in this regard went far beyond mere athletic accomplishment. The success of so many Jewish champions and contenders challenged anti-Semitic stereotypes and helped shape a Jewish American identity.

Like their Irish and Italian counterparts—and the Afro-American and Latino boxers who would later take their place in the boxing pantheon—most Jewish boxers were a product of impoverished inner city ghettos. It was no coincidence that from 1890 to 1950 the majority of Jewish boxers came from New York City, home to the largest and poorest Jewish community in the United States. Harry Haft, speaking only Yiddish, would have no problem being accepted and understood the very first time he stepped into New York's legendary Stillman's Gym.

The first five decades of the twentieth century represented a golden age for boxing. The sport played a significant role in the popular culture of the day. Millions of fans listened to important fights over the radio and—beginning in the late 1940s—watched them on television. They followed the exploits of their favorite boxers in the daily newspapers and in movie newsreels. Heavyweight title fights, especially those involving Jack Dempsey in the 1920s, or Joe Louis a decade later, would sometimes take on the magnitude of a presidential election.

In the years leading up to World War II, as the hardships of the Depression eased, the number of Jewish boxers began to decline.

Nonetheless, they remained an important presence in the postwar boxing scene, especially in New York City.

Harry was in the right place to start his professional boxing career. New York City was still the epicenter of the boxing universe (as it had been since the 1920s) in terms of money, activity, and importance. It also had the best trainers and gyms.

In 1948, approximately one thousand professional boxers were licensed in New York State. A dozen boxing arenas, including the fabled Madison Square Garden, operated on a regular basis within a ten-mile radius of Manhattan.* Harry fought in many of them including the Coney Island Velodrome and Eastern Parkway Arena in Brooklyn, the Jamaica Arena in Queens, Westchester County Center in White Plains, and the Staten Island Stadium. Harry would also fight in Rochester and Binghamton, New York; Miami Beach and Jacksonville, Florida; Wilkes-Barre, Pennsylvania; Paterson, New Jersey; and Providence, Rhode Island.

The late 1940s was to be the last hurrah for the golden age of boxing in America. Demographic, economic, and societal changes had already begun to affect the sport. With the economy continuing to improve, jobs and career opportunities opened up for many young men who might otherwise have considered a career in the prize ring. In addition, five million veterans took advantage of the G.I. Bill and the chance for a free college or technical education.

The postwar movement of boxing's (mostly white) core customers from the cities to the suburbs was also hurting the network

---

*In 2005 there were only ninety-eight professional boxers licensed in New York State and barely thirty promotions for the year. New York City has long since given up its title as boxing capital of the world.

of small arenas that relied on their patronage to stay in business. These "fight clubs," as they are known in the boxing vernacular, were also profoundly affected by the new medium of television, which began saturating the airwaves with boxing up to six nights a week. Many fans chose to stay home, preferring to watch the free TV fights (not to mention Milton Berle's Texaco Star Theater and the Jackie Gleason Show) from the comfort of their living rooms. At the same time, the growing popularity of other professional sports, such as basketball and football, was yet another factor contributing to boxing's eventual demise as a mainstream sport.

Television was both good and bad for boxing. It was creating millions of new fans but boxing's greedy and shortsighted moguls were exploiting the popularity of the sport at the expense of its fading infrastructure. With the closure of so many small arenas all over the country, boxing's farm system for developing new talent was being decimated. Between 1949 and 1951, scores of fight clubs went out of business and those that remained struggled to survive. Within a few years, professional boxing shows had ceased to exist in most of the arenas and cities that Harry Haft had appeared in.

The demand for talent created by the ravenous TV schedule soon outran the supply, with the result that many young fighters were being rushed into main events against experienced opponents before they had a chance to develop their skills. Compounding boxing's problems at this crucial juncture in its history was the damage inflicted on it through the ever-present curse of criminal infiltration.

Gamblers and gangsters have always been attracted to professional boxing. The history of underworld influence within the sport is long and sordid—so long and so sordid that it is hard to imagine one without the other.

The fight game is an enterprise closer to show business than to other professional sports. Boxers are independent contractors who actually have very little independence when it comes to controlling the direction of their careers. Often they are at the mercy of unscrupulous promoters, crooked or incompetent managers, and negligent state boxing commissions. They are easily exploited. To this day professional boxing has no national commissioner, union, or responsible centralized authority.

In the early 1930s New York bootleggers Owney Madden and Bill Duffy were the undercover managers of several top fighters including future heavyweight champion of the world, Primo Carnera. The 6' 6", 270-pound Carnera, a former circus strongman, was a fighter of modest skills and, despite his huge size, could barely break an egg with his muscle-bound punches. But after winning a series of fixed fights he was moved to the top of the heavyweight ranks. In a bout many boxing historians believe to have been prearranged (without Carnera's knowledge) he won the heavyweight championship in 1933 by knocking out Jack Sharkey.

Shortly after losing his title to Max Baer in 1934 in a fight that was not fixed, Carnera was abandoned by the mob, his usefulness as a cash cow depleted. He left boxing virtually penniless, having been totally fleeced by the hoodlums who controlled his career. Luckier than most mob-managed fighters, Carnera later found new fame and financial security as a professional wrestler and actor.

With the end of Prohibition in 1933 mob interest in big-time boxing accelerated. By the late 1940s several organized crime figures had successfully infiltrated boxing's most powerful promotional organization the International Boxing Club (IBC). The IBC was the exclusive promoter of boxing at Madison Square Garden, the Chicago Stadium, Detroit Olympia, and the St. Louis Arena. The criminals behind the IBC often used their power to buy into, or simply take over, the management of many of boxing's top contenders and champions.

By 1949 the only arenas showing any consistent profits were those being subsidized with television money. With the downsizing of boxing's grassroots structure, and TV's growing influence over the sport, legitimate managers were experiencing difficulty in finding work for their fighters. A choice had to be made to either approach someone with "connections" to the lucrative TV market and the big-time arenas, or risk being frozen out. A good number of legitimate managers saw the writing on the wall and simply chose to leave the business.

A new breed of manager was now gaining entré to the sport. Many were cronies and associates of the behind-the-scenes lowlifes involved with the IBC. Crowding out the legitimate managers, who came up through the ranks and knew the game inside out, were garment center entrepreneurs, restaurant owners, bookmakers, and small-time hoodlums. What they all had in common, other than a desire to be part of the glamour and excitement of the sport, was a complete lack of knowledge as to how to properly manage a professional fighter. Most of them were simply fronts for the crooks who were their silent partners in the ownership of professional boxers.

The savvy, old-school managers who stayed with the game understood the landscape. Refusal to hand over a promising prospect, or an established contender, to a "connected" manager could result in the fighter's being blacklisted and thereby denied important and lucrative matches.

One of the most blatant examples of mob influence in boxing

during this era was the Billy Fox vs. Jake LaMotta bout on November 14, 1947, in New York's Madison Square Garden. Despite being the number one ranked middleweight contender for four straight years, LaMotta had been unable to secure a championship match because of his refusal to give up control of his career to Frankie Carbo, the notorious underworld figure who was the power behind the IBC. Finally, desperate for a title bout, he reluctantly agreed to the mob's request that he throw his fight with Fox in exchange for a shot at the middleweight championship.

Fox defeated LaMotta by a technical knockout in the fourth round. Jake's act was unconvincing. Everyone believed he had thrown the fight, but it could not be proven until thirteen years later when, testifying before a U. S. Senate Committee investigating boxing, LaMotta admitted what had already been suspected—that he threw the Fox fight.

Not surprisingly, Carbo's lieutenant, Philadelphia mobster Frank "Blinky" Palermo, managed Billy Fox. At the time, Fox had a record of forty-nine knockouts in fifty victories. It was common knowledge that Palermo had fixed many of his fights.

It should be noted that although the vast majority of bouts were fought on the level, there was enough extortion, monopoly, and corruption at the highest levels of the sport, to bring about a full-scale Congressional investigation into boxing in the 1950s. Legendary sportswriter Jimmy Cannon was right on the money when he called professional boxing, "the red light district of sports."

After years of stealing from just about everyone connected to the sport, arranging fixed fights and generally corrupting and abusing professional boxing Frankie Carbo (the "underworld commissioner of boxing") and Frank "Blinky" Palermo were finally convicted, in 1961, of extortion while trying to muscle their way into the management of welterweight champion Don Jordan. Carbo received a 25-year jail sentence. He died in 1976. Palermo received 15 years which he began serving in 1964. Upon his release from prison in 1978 he had the chutzpah to apply for a boxing manager's license even while one of his accusers was still in the witness protection program! After an outcry in the press Palermo was denied the license but he continued to stay around the fringes of the sport and was believed to control certain fighters right up to his death in 1995 at the age of 91. The following short bios are of world boxing figures mentioned in Alan Haft's book:

Eddie Coco, a New York hoodlum and Carbo associate, owned "a piece" of middleweight champion Rocky Graziano. (In this book, Coco claims he could get $30,000 for Harry's contract.) In 1951, during an argument with a parking lot attendant, the hot-tempered Coco pulled out a gun and shot him dead. Coco was sentenced to life in prison.

The 125th Street Gym referred to in this book, where Harry met Bill "Pop" Miller, was known as the Uptown Gym and was located on the second floor of the famous Apollo Theater in Harlem. The entrance was just to the side of the ticket booth. The gym closed in 1962.

Coley Wallace, the gentleman boxer who befriended Harry Haft in New York, was eventually taken over by Palermo. "He ruined boxing for me," said Wallace in an interview in 2000. Wallace claimed that he got just $3,000 of the $20,000 purse he was promised for fighting Ezzard Charles and that he didn't get paid at all after beating Bill Gilliam at the Eastern Parkway Arena. Like many other main-bout fighters controlled by Palermo he retired from boxing with little money to show for it and regretting the day he ever met the hoodlum. A gracious and friendly man, who greeted all his friends with a hug, Wallace was one of the most beloved and popular ex-fighters on the New York scene. He portrayed Joe Louis in the 1953 movie based on Louis's life. Coley Wallace passed away in January 2005 at the age of seventy-seven.

Charley Goldman, the wizened old Yoda-like trainer who always wore a derby and instructed Harry for the Marciano fight, was one of boxing's greatest trainers. Charley, who was born in Russia in 1888, came to this country while still a tot. Standing 5'1" and weighing 115 pounds in his prime, Goldman fought close to two hundred professional bouts from 1904 to 1914, meeting many of the world's top bantamweight fighters. He became a trainer in the 1920s. Four of his fighters won world championships, including, in 1952, his prize pupil, Rocky Marciano, the only undefeated heavyweight champion. Goldman was the only trainer that shrewd boxing manager Al Weill employed to train his fighters. He died in New York on November 15, 1968.

Rocky Marciano was in the process of developing into a great fighter at the time he fought Harry Haft in 1949. Marciano had the advantage of learning from one of boxing's top trainers, Charley Goldman, and of being guided by its shrewdest manager, Al Weill. One can only speculate what Harry's boxing career might have looked like had he been so fortunate. Marciano, a boxing legend, is still the only heavyweight champion to retire undefeated, having won all forty-nine of his professional bouts, forty-three by knockout. He died in a plane crash in 1969, one day shy of his forty-sixth birthday.

Artie Levine was a talented boxer-puncher and world-ranked contender who had the misfortune of being managed by mobsters.

After being sent while suffering with a fever into the ring against another mob-controlled fighter, Billy Fox, Levine became fed up with the business and retired in 1949 at the age of twenty-four.

Harold Green was a top welterweight and middleweight contender during the mid- to late 1940s. He defeated future middleweight champion Rocky Graziano twice via ten-round decisions. In their next fight, in 1945, Green was knocked out in the third round. Years later Green claimed he threw the fight when mobsters promised him a future title bout if he agreed to lose to Graziano. The title fight never materialized.

Morris "Whitey" Bimstein was one of boxing's legendary trainers, whose career spanned the 1920s to the 1960s. Born in New York's Lower East Side, Bimstein worked the corners of dozens of world champions and countless other fighters. He was considered one of the best "cut men" in the business. At various times he partnered with two other legendary trainers, Ray Arcel and Freddie Brown. He died in 1969 at the age seventy-two.

Bill "Pop" Miller, originally from the West Indies, began his career as a trainer in the early 1900s. He worked with champions "Tiger" Flowers, "Panama" Al Brown, and Primo Carnera in the 1920s and 1930's. The beret-wearing Miller, considered one of the best trainers in New York, was known for his acerbic personality and boxing smarts. He established a relationship with Blinky Palermo and often steered fighters, one of whom was Coley Wallace, to the Philadelphia mobster. He passed away in 1958, age unknown.

Freddie Brown, with his flattened nose and ever-present cigar looked like the quintessential boxing trainer. He was one of about a dozen outstanding New York Jewish trainers who were active in boxing from the 1920s to the 1950s. Himself an ex-fighter, Brown trained hundreds of fighters but is best remembered as a cut man for Rocky Marciano and as co-trainer, with Ray Arcel, of Roberto Duran. He died in 1986.

"Slapsie" Maxie Rosenbloom, light heavyweight champion of the world from 1930 to 1934, engaged in nearly three hundred professional fights from 1923 to 1939. After he retired from boxing, Maxie built a second successful career in Hollywood as a character actor appearing in more than a hundred films. He died in 1976 at the age of seventy-two.

Roland LaStarza, handsome and college-educated, was undefeated in thirty-seven fights when he lost a controversial split ten-round decision to Rocky Marciano in March 1950—nine months after his bout with Harry Haft. Three and a half years later LaStarza attempted to take the heavyweight championship from Marciano, who was defending his newly won crown for the second time, and was knocked out in the eleventh round. After fighting sporadically over the next five years, he finally retired in 1959.

Lew Stillman, the gruff curmudgeon who owned the world famous New York Gym that bore his name, once estimated that thirty thousand fighters worked out in his gym during the forty years of its operation. Stillman sold the gym in 1959, and it closed down two years later.

Harry Mandell was a small-time manager who had little success in the fight business. (Anyone willing to pay the $15.00 licensing fee to the State Athletic Commission could become a fight manager—at least in name.) The mark of a successful manager lies in his ability to match his fighter properly. In this regard Harry Haft did not get the best of advice or direction from Mandell judging by the fact that after barely a dozen victories he began meeting, and losing to, far more experienced fighters.

HARRY HAFT

The Threat

BY THE SUMMER OF 1949, Rocky Marciano, the future un-defeated heavyweight champion of the world, had knocked out all sixteen of the fighters he had faced. Now, on the night of July 18 in the Rhode Island Auditorium in Providence there was every indication that Marciano would continue his run of victories in the ten-round bout with Harry Haft.

Rocky's reputation as a fearsome puncher was growing. Yet Harry Haft was not afraid.

Harry was known as an action fighter who liked to wade in and deliver punches. He didn't worry much about finesse or style. He knew that after he got hit hard, he would lose control and forget what he had learned in the gym anyway. All of his handlers recognized his punching ability and tried to teach him boxing, but he was a lousy pupil. Some of the best trainers gave him a look. Whitey Bimstein, Bill Miller, and now, oddly enough, Marciano's own trainer, Charley Goldman, had trained him for this fight.

Harry knew that Marciano would not be afraid to slug it out with him. Harry didn't mind being the underdog and was confident that he had trained hard and he could beat Rocky.

He didn't allow thoughts of losing. His career was on the line because of a string of tough losses, mostly fights stopped for eye cuts, and as a last desperate measure he had been hypnotized into thinking that Rocky's punches could not hurt him and that he would not bleed.

Only he knew the real reason why he continued fighting. Boxing put his name in the newspapers. It was a way of telling the world that he was alive, that he had survived the concentration camps. With his name prominent in the newspapers, he hoped, family and friends would find him. And, most important, that Leah would find him, too.

Harry was twenty-four. He never forgot Leah, the girl he was about to marry at sixteen, just days before he was sent to his first slave labor camp. Thoughts of her buoyed him through the darkness of his journeys to the camps on cattle cars. Now he dreamed of becoming famous enough so that if she were alive, she would find him. This was a fight that he had to win.

Harry and his manager, Harry Mandell, "the other Harry," had walked the half-mile to the auditorium a little after seven that evening. The fight with Marciano was to be the last of the night, the main event. Four preliminary bouts came first, and both Harrys expected to be in the ring by 10:00.

It was about 9:00 when three strange men entered Haft's dressing room. They came in politely enough while Harry was sitting up on the massage table talking fight strategy with Mandell.

Mandell was seated in front of the table on a wooden folding chair. It was warm in the room. Mandell had taken off his suit jacket and hung it on the back of the chair. His collar was open and his tie knot was loosened. There was tension in the air.

"Hershel," Mandell said, "we're gonna stay away from this guy's right hand . . . and you'll hit and run . . ."

The strangers approached, and Mandell jumped to his feet.

"Hey, who are you guys?" he said. "Nobody's allowed in here except fighters and their managers, and whoever else I let in."

One of the men stepped forward. He was in a suit and tie, and held his hat in his hands when he spoke. "Where do you think you are?" he replied. "We're in charge around here. Take a walk, and take him too. I wanna talk to your fighter alone." He motioned to Mandell and the handler who was there to warm up Harry and handle cuts.

"No fucking way. I'm not going anywhere. Whatever you got to say to my fighter, you can say to me," said Mandell, planting his feet.

One of the other men, short, and heavyset, walked the cut man to the door leading out of the room.

"Come back later," the fat man said, and pushed him out the door, closing it behind him and now standing guard.

The third stranger grabbed the folding chair, flipped it around, and sat down, draping his arms over the chair back. He lifted his hands to hold the hat and suit jacket for the guy in charge.

"You can stay if you insist."

Harry Haft was already in his purple trunks and shoes, and had a big towel draped around his neck. He played with the tape that had just been wrapped around his hands.

"What's your business here?" Haft asked, his thick accent not giving away any fear.

"Boys, here's the problem. We're here to protect Rocky."

Mandell spit on the floor before answering, "Well I'm here to protect Harry Haft!" Mandell was no stranger to threats.

"Take your muscle out of here."

"Well, you don't have much to protect," he pointed to Haft. "He needs to go down in the first round."

Haft got off the table and stood face to face with the man in charge. "Fuck you. You don't scare me. The Germans tried to tell me what to do, and I'm still around."

"We know all about you. Don't get smart with us. We mean what we say. You know Vince Foster?"

Haft looked at Mandell. Mandell spoke. "Sure, I heard of him."

"We told him not to beat Tony Pellone in the Garden, but he didn't listen. Vince was a tough guy too. Now he's dead."

"He's dead?" Haft said, looking at Mandell.

On January 14, 1949, Vince Foster, a welterweight from Omaha, Nebraska made ring headlines when he knocked out the heavily favored New Yorker, Tony Pellone, in Madison Square Garden.

What Mandell and Haft could not know was that at 1:30 that morning, Vince Foster was crushed to death in an automobile crash.

"Do what you're told and you'll live to read about it in tomorrow's paper," said the muscle guy on the folding chair.

The third man hanging at the door said, "Chicky, we gotta go. The Bell-Firpo fight's over."

"Do what you're told if you want to live," said the man they called Chicky.

Just like that, Haft and Mandell were alone in the room.

"He's dead? What's this talk about Vince Foster?" Haft asked.

Mandell shrugged his shoulders.

"What should I do?" implored Haft.

The other Harry lifted his eyebrows and threw his hands up in frustration and disgust. "I don't know what you want me to tell you," he said.

"But you're my manager," said Harry.

"I don't know. I just don't know," Mandell said.

Haft took the towel off his neck and threw it on the floor. He lay back down on the massage table and closed his eyes. All the years of struggle to stay alive flashed through his brain. All the dead corpses. All the killing. And now, the thought that they might kill him enraged him.

"Not here in America," he thought "Not over a prizefight!"

The door to the dressing room opened. In came the cut man. "You guys ready? It's time. Let me grab my stuff."

Haft sat up, checked the lacing on his shoes. Mandell grabbed the boxing gloves and helped him slip them on. He tied them tightly. Haft pounded his fists together, deep in thought, and his life passed before him.

PART ONE

NIGHTMARES

Born Lucky

HARRY HAFT came into the world on July 28, 1925, in a small town in Poland in the vicinity of Piotrkow, just south of Lodz. Belchatow had ten thousand citizens, working mostly in and around the weaving and textile trades. It had once been a predominantly Jewish shtetl known for its central market, where weavers, shoemakers, hatters, and shopkeepers sold their wares to local farmers. By 1925, following World War I and the formation of an independent Polish state, Belchatow had modernized into a city, with several mechanized factories and mills and with an evenly divided population of Jews and gentiles.

It was anything but good fortune to be born a Jew in Poland in 1925, though, and Harry would think back on his birth as his first act of survival in an increasingly miserable time.

• • •

"Hertzka," his mother would scold him, "no complaints from the boy who was born lucky."

She was, of course referring to his birth.

Hynda Haft was tall and strong. She was an energetic, hardworking, and cheerful woman despite the terrible poverty the family endured. Yet, though poor, she was so fat that she did not even realize she was pregnant with her eighth child. When Harry

9

was born, he came unannounced, while Hynda was stooped over a basin scrubbing clothes on a washboard. She barely noticed what she thought was a gas pain, and she continued working. As she stooped over to catch a breath, Harry dropped from her and landed headfirst on the hard wooden floor.

With her height, the fall could have killed him, but aside from a small bruise on his forehead, Harry was unhurt. For years his brothers and sisters would often excuse his odd behavior and dogged stubbornness by recalling that he began his life with a bump on his head.

Hynda was happy to have the baby survive, though he would be another mouth to feed and another body to clothe. Harry was her last child, and he liked to think of himself as her favorite.

The Hafts were a close, large family of ten trying to endure the hardships and poverty of the time. His four brothers and three sisters would play different roles in his life. Aria, the oldest brother, would become his father figure and chief tormentor, Rosa, the sister who would mother and abandon him; sisters Brandel and Rifka and brothers Machel and Birach would share the ongoing family struggle, while Peretz would be part of Harry's soul as the brother sharing the fight to stay alive in Auschwitz-Birkenau.

Harry's father, Moishe Haft, was a tiny and frail man. Hynda and Moishe made an odd-looking couple. Their pairing was the result of an arranged marriage, and they met for the first time on their wedding day. Such a coupling was easily explained when the poor were matched with the poor.

Moishe was gentle and quiet by nature and did his best to squeeze out a meager living for his large family. He would hitch a horse to a wagon and deliver fruits and vegetables from the local farmers to neighboring towns, leaving early in the morning and

Aria Haft *(left)*, Harry's oldest brother, before the war. Courtesy of the author. Peretz Haft, Harry's brother and fellow concentration camp survivor. Courtesy of Arthur Haft.

returning exhausted late at night. All his hard work could not change the fact that in Belchatow, the Hafts were among the poorest of the poor, living in a shanty near the center of town in the midst of a busy farmer's market that drew crowds of people three or four days a week. There were three rooms for the ten of them, and all beds were shared. In the winter, all ten would huddle together in the kitchen to sleep on bedding covering the floor near the stove. On one side of the house, the roof and several walls had caved in. When the weather was nice, a cool breeze could flow throughout, but in the winter there was little difference between the temperature outside and the temperature inside.

Harry felt as if he lived in a jungle. The family behaved like pack animals, sleeping in groups to ward off the cold, with the cub moving from bed to bed, to wherever another warm body was welcomed.

Meat was scarce at mealtime, and the family subsisted mostly on potatoes and overripe fruits and vegetables that remained unsold on Moishe's wagon.

Unknown to Harry, the early poverty was a blessing in disguise, for he became accustomed to hard living conditions at an early age. He was remarkably mature at age three, and he liked to walk out the door of his house to wander the streets of Belchatow unsupervised. He became a favorite at the market, where he liked to play with the stray cats and dogs prowling for food scraps and water on the ground.

As an adult, Harry would struggle to remember his father. His mother never blamed him for his father's death, and his siblings would not put that thought to words, though some may have felt otherwise. Later, it would sicken him that his only remaining vision of Moishe was cast in a shroud of death, a death brought on by the germs of typhoid fever that Harry, the baby, was the first to contract. No one knew how Harry could have picked up the germ. He could have caught it anywhere in his wanderings about town. His mother blamed herself for dressing him in the leftovers donated by more fortunate Jewish families, clothes that looked clean but that she had not first washed.

Hynda was the next to get the fever, while she nursed Harry. Moishe caught the disease from her. Unlike Hynda and Harry, who were both built big and strong, Moishe was overcome by the fever after a brief week of sweats. He was brought to a hospital for treatment, but there was only enough money to keep him in the hospital for two days. He was then sent home with instructions for home care.

Hynda made a bed out of blankets and rags for him on the floor of the kitchen. It was winter, and the family tried to keep him warm by feeding the fire in the stove day and night. To no avail, the fever worsened. Harry remembers the feeling of helplessness waiting for his father to die.

Still able to talk, but very weak with fever, Moishe asked everyone to leave the kitchen except Aria and Hynda.

Hynda would bear witness to the conversation. She would later tell all the brothers and sisters what their father had said to Aria.

"Aria, come close," Moishe whispered. "Aria, you will have to be a father to my children."

Aria began to cry.

"Be strong. Promise me you will be lenient toward your brothers and sisters."

"I will. I will." sobbed Aria.

"And you cannot leave and marry until all your brothers and sisters are married."

Aria silently assured his father that he would take his place in the family. He had little choice but to give this promise if he wished his father to die in peace.

The next morning, Moishe did not wake up.

Three-year-old Harry stood over his father, not comprehending, not crying.

The family wrapped Moishe in sheets and put him in his empty delivery wagon. His faithful horse took him to the cemetery, with Aria holding the reins while the family and several friends followed behind. Unable to afford a casket or headstone, the Haft family arrived unceremoniously at the graveyard and buried him there.

Aria was sixteen years old and now the head of the household. Harry was the youngest child, and he would come to know the depths of the buried resentment Aria felt about his new burden.

Before long, the family fell apart. Brandel, Rifka, and Rosa left their mother to find work cleaning houses in Lodz. While there, Rosa would become involved with a married man, Peretz Kolton. Peretz had the reputation of being a playboy, and so to avoid bigamy prosecution and social disapproval, the young lovers escaped to Russia.

Everyone in the family had to work, and by the time Harry was five, he too had a job. On market days, Harry's mother would wake him early so that he could walk to market square and hang around the poultry market, where he would do his business. Unlike other children, he did not have time to be fascinated by the stacked cages full of squawking geese and chickens. Harry, at five, knew these animals brought an opportunity to earn the equivalent of a penny or two, to buy bread for the family.

The Jewish women, who would buy live geese or chickens to be slaughtered by a rabbi, were his customers.

Harry was a fast walker, and a reliable means of transportation to get the live poultry and fowl to their destiny. The women would make their purchase and Harry would stuff the bird under his arm, or on a busy day, one under each arm, and make haste down the road to the slaughterhouse, a few miles away, at the outskirts of town.

When Harry would return with the freshly butchered kill, he would be paid for his efforts. He never thought about the life and death of the poultry, but always focused on the fresh rolls that could be purchased with the money he earned.

Apart from market days, Harry went to public school where Jews and gentiles learned together. Later in the day he would attend religious school at a local synagogue.

Harry had difficulty in both schools. In religious school, the fact that he had no father and was poor was an invitation for neglect by the rabbi. However, it was in the mixed public school where he had real trouble.

The Christian children came into school with the idea that the Jews killed their God, an idea that was commonly voiced in church sermons. There were so many fights in school about this subject that it seemed normal. Harry also felt that some of the resentment came from the fact that Jews in Belchatow owned most of the factories where the Christian children's parents worked.

In the early elementary grades, Harry's teachers were predominantly women. The female teachers were not as openly anti-Semitic toward the Jewish children as the male teachers Harry would encounter in later grades. In fact, some of the female teachers were kind and tender toward him. The male teachers in the upper grades were less kind. They applied a harsher standard of discipline to the Jewish children, and this standard applied to academics as well as behavior.

One day a male teacher asked, "Harry, who was the first king of Poland?"

Harry did not know the answer, and he was paddled on the spot.

The teacher then asked the same question to a non-Jewish student, who also did not know the answer. No punishment followed.

There were youth gangs who terrorized the Jewish children. Harry understood early that he needed to fight and get a reputation as a fighter so that he would not be their victim. He had his share of fights in school and he never backed away. There came a day when his reputation was finally established enough to protect him from harm.

Harry's fiery temper boiled over in a soccer game in the

schoolyard. Jews and non-Jews never played on the same side, always against each other. Harry was handling the ball when a defender started kicking him in the legs.

He knew that in soccer you can get your legs kicked unintentionally when going for the ball. However, when it keeps happening, something else is going on.

The kicking led to pushing and shoving, and a fight broke out. The two boys were the same size and age, but Harry was the tougher scrapper and was getting the better of the fight. Just then a male teacher came over to break it up.

Harry was on top of the boy when the teacher grabbed him by his neck and pulled him off. The teacher slapped Harry a couple of times to try to calm him down. Harry swung back at the teacher. This time the teacher grabbed Harry by his shirt collar hard enough to hurt. Harry came back to his senses and tried to explain about the repeated kicking in the game.

The teacher began shaking him.

"You are all killers," the teacher screamed in Harry's face.

Harry knew he meant "Christ killers," a common anti-Semitic taunt. Harry was not able to control his raging temper.

He wrestled free of the teacher's grip, picked up a rock the size of his hand, and threw it with all his might point-blank at his teacher's head.

The teacher threw up his arms and managed to deflect the rock with his hand. Other teachers ran over to help him. It took the combined force of three teachers to restrain Harry.

This episode ended Harry's public education. The school expelled him on the spot, and he was held away from the other children until Aria came to get him. As he led Harry away from the school, the older brother raged with anger. He refused to hear a word of Harry's explanation.

When they were a short distance from the school, Aria began pummeling Harry with his fists. Harry tried to shield himself from the blows, so Aria threw him to the ground and kicked him. He finally paused and told his brother to get up.

The boys continued to walk home. Every hundred yards or so, it seemed some new thought would anger Aria, and he would slap Harry in the back of the head. Sometimes he slapped his brother so hard that Harry fell to the ground. Another kick would follow before Aria allowed Harry to get up.

From that day forward, Aria's beatings never seemed to stop. Harry became his problem child, and he was determined to straighten him out.

Aria immediately put his belligerent young brother to work. Aria taught Harry to hand weave, and from then on Harry's workday began at 4:30 A.M.

Harry soon learned that if he refused to get up, he would be beaten. When he did work, he was given bread and potatoes to eat. He had little choice.

The Occupation

EARLY IN 1939, when news of the Third Reich's invasion of Czechoslovakia reached Belchatow, life forever changed. Poland began to prepare for a German offensive. Aria was conscripted into the Polish army, and his unit was immediately sent off to protect the border from the expected incursion of German troops. Hynda and fourteen-year-old Harry were the only ones left in the house.

In early September 1939, the bombing of Belchatow began. The city center was heavily hit, and the explosions were so close to their shanty that Harry and his mother left the city and headed for the farmland near the outskirts of town. Harry hitched the horse to the delivery wagon and drove his mother off amidst explosions, smoke, fire, and dust. He steered the wagon out of town to a familiar fruit orchard in the countryside, stopping briefly along the road to give the horse a rest. Harry helped his mother out of the wagon and found a stretch of grass where they could rest and enjoy a momentary feeling of safety.

Soon the air filled with the gentle hum of an engine that steadily grew louder. Harry turned his face up to the sky and tried to find the source of the sound. He was startled by the sight of a low-flying airplane with a swastika painted on the side.

The plane passed directly above them and continued flying

south. Before it disappeared, the plane made a wide turn, and they watched as it began to head back in their direction.

They climbed back on the cart and urged the horse on. Before they had moved a hundred yards, bullets rained down upon them. The horse was hit and went wild with panic, overturning the cart and throwing Hynda and Harry to the ground.

They ran toward the tallest and thickest trees in the orchard. The plane made another deliberate turn and came back, this time trying to shoot them as they ran. Luckily, they were able to reach safety. They didn't dare leave that spot for fear of becoming a target again.

In the morning they abandoned their horse and wagon and walked back to town, carrying as many green apples as they could manage. When they reached their house, they were happy to see that it was still standing, although there was rubble all around. The city center was mostly destroyed.

A few days later the remnants of the Polish army unit from Belchatow began trickling home. There, among the wounded and beaten, was Aria, resembling a walking skeleton. Harry and Hynda were overcome with joy to see Aria walk through the door, and they nursed him back to health with potatoes and bread.

On October 5, 1939, the last major unit of the Polish army surrendered, and the German occupation of Belchatow began. "Folk Germans" that is, Germans born in Poland welcomed Hitler's troops, who in turn came to rely heavily on these citizens to accomplish the Germanization of Poland. This assistance was particularly displayed in Belchatow, home to German textile designers, engineers, and tradesmen. There was a whole neighborhood of local Germans who spoke their native tongue and attended the

Lutheran church and schools even as they worked in Jewish-owned factories.

The city was soon divided into Jewish and gentile sectors and annexed with other land into West Poland, then incorporated under the Third Reich. A new German city government was formed and a Folk German mayor was quickly appointed. In short order, Jewish houses, property, and businesses were seized. Thus began the dark days for the Jews, as the new government passed anti-Jewish measures.

Jews were systematically picked off the streets for forced labor. Jews were allowed to walk only in the middle of the road, Synagogues were destroyed, and all Jews were made to wear the yellow Star of David on their clothing. Jewish bank accounts were frozen. Jews were forbidden to travel and subjected to a curfew.

Harry Haft, now fifteen, was an eyewitness to the beatings, torture, and murder of his friends and neighbors. He would see beatings in the public square for any small violation of the new rules, and it frightened him.

He learned from observation that the Germans knew how to inflict pain. They could beat and practically kill a man, but keep him alive while he wished for death.

Although Belchatow was now part of Germany, Piotrkow, about ten miles to the east, was still considered to be part of Poland, now a German protectorate. Aria still had customers in Piotrkow, but now it was illegal to cross the border.

Aria organized a small group of men to smuggle goods across the border, where they could be sold at a very high profit. Aria received the goods on credit from acquaintances having the raw materials. Harry and the others were the mules. Their job was to strap the goods on their backs and travel at night through the fields, avoiding the guarded roads, to deliver the bounty to buyers in Piotrkow. The immediate danger for the smugglers came from farmers' dogs.

Aria controlled all the money from the smuggling operation, and he gave Harry no choice but to participate. Their brother Peretz would also secure goods for Harry to take over the border to sell, but he himself never risked the crossing.

One night, two German soldiers were waiting with their rifles for Harry and the other runners. The soldiers caught sight of them in the moonlight and ordered them to stop. They fired, and the smugglers dropped their parcels and ran.

Harry kept on running with his package still secured. A bullet hit him in the side, but he knew he had to keep running until he got back to Aria.

The Jewish population was forced to live in a small section of town. The sense of despair and poverty was shared by all. The exposure to cold, hunger, and overcrowding caused an epidemic of typhus in the Jewish zone. It raged out of control without proper supervision from Jewish doctors, some of whom had escaped earlier, while others had been killed for ministering to their people.

Strangely, the Hafts found themselves prospering as never before. Aria's smuggling operation provided them with more money than they could spend. Their small house was filled with food not just bread and potatoes, but meats and fruits and candies.

During this time Hynda was now in a position to help others. Relatives and friends who were hungry or needy were taken in. Harry's mother sent provisions to cousins who were unable to come in person, and she returned many past favors from neighbors by giving them money.

One day, Harry returned home from a visit with friends in the zone to a loud commotion in front of his house. The yelling and arguing of a dozen strange men enveloped him. In the midst of the ruckus, it appeared to Harry that Aria was fighting it out with the leader of a rival group of smugglers. Aria's opponent was the father of a girl Harry dated. This man had his brother in a tight bear hug, with Aria struggling wildly to break free.

Believing that his brother was being overpowered by the larger man, Harry instinctively broke through the crowd, grabbed the man by his shirt collar, and pulled him off Aria. The man turned and faced Harry squarely. Harry threw a punch to the man's jaw that dropped him to the ground. Blood poured from his mouth.

The man dragged his wrist across his bloody face. Dazed, he sat on his haunches and shook his head. Everyone stopped arguing, and the man mumbled some words to Harry that were hard to understand until he spit out several teeth.

Everyone was stunned by Harry's behavior. Aria looked on in shock, amazed not by the fact that Harry had come to his rescue but that he packed so much rage and power in his punch.

Harry looked around at the circle of men, and with a bold grin asked, "Who wants me next?"

Not a man stepped forward, but a stranger did speak.

"Two nights ago, the Germans were waiting for us on our way out of town," he said.

"So?" asked Harry.

"They killed one of our men. We think someone tipped them off."

Aria started to react again.

"You know we would never, never do something like that!"

Harry would soon learn that he had made a terrible mistake.

These accusations had made Aria fighting mad, and the man he hit, his girlfriend's father, was not the accuser. In fact, he was holding Aria back from fighting. The crowd soon broke up. Harry rubbed his hand, which was hurting. It felt as if he had broken some of his knuckles. He looked up and found Aria staring at him. If he expected an apology for the mistake, Harry was not giving one, not to Aria or to his girl's father.

Aria took a couple of steps toward Harry. Harry did not back up but remained stubborn and on guard. He did not wait for his brother to speak, but pointed his finger at Aria and said, "Don't you dare lift your hand to me. Don't ever think you can do it."

Harry could see in his eyes that the silent Aria was proud of him. He hoped that Aria was thinking about all the times Harry took it without fighting back. Perhaps he understood at that moment that Harry had always restrained himself and given him the respect he would have shown a father. Harry knew that their relationship would never be the same, and he knew that Aria would never hit him again.

Captured

ALTHOUGH HARRY MISSED seeing Leah terribly, it took him more than a week to summon up the courage to call on her and apologize to her father. To ensure his welcome, he carried several loaves of bread, some potatoes, and a cabbage with him. He knocked on the door with some trepidation and was surprised when a strange man answered.

"Who are you?" he asked, eyeing the food in Harry's arms.

"I've got something for Meir," Harry answered.

The stranger moved aside from the doorway and let Harry enter.

"I am Schmuel," he said. "I am Meir's brother."

"Hertzka Haft," extending his hand and trying not to drop the food at the same time.

"You," said Meir, as he spotted him from the end of the hallway. "What balls you have to come here."

"I came to apologize. I have brought some food."

Food was in short supply. Harry felt that Meir would have to accept the offering and be civil about the apology.

"I would like to continue seeing your daughter," Harry told Meir in a brave tone.

"And why should I let my daughter see such a hothead?"

"Sir," Harry reasoned, "I am the kind of man who would do anything to protect his family. Would you not do the same?

"You know the Germans have taken all the tools from the Jewish dentists. Thanks to you, my mouth will never be the same."

Meir turned to Schmuel who was already taking the food from Harry.

"Schmuel, what do you think? Do you think we have here a good young man or a bad guy for Leah?"

"He is a good guy," answered Schmuel. "He has food, and we are hungry."

"All right, I will go find Leah and tell her that her good guy named Hertzka Haft has come calling."

Leah came in from the next room, overjoyed to see Harry.

All the ugliness in Harry's world disappeared when the beautiful Leah appeared. At fourteen, she was slightly taller than Harry, and her long, dark, curly hair framed her face gracefully. She spoke in a soft voice and had muscular slender arms.

She walked over to Harry and gave him a long hug, but no kiss, since her father was watching.

"May I take her out?" Harry asked Meir.

"Where are you going? It is dangerous out there."

"I will bring her back safely."

Meir relented. It was still early, the middle of a warm sunny day, and he felt guilty denying his daughter. He didn't question further where they were going.

Harry knew of a safe passage to a secret place of peace and beauty. It was along the smuggler's trail, and it led to the Rakowka River. He found a secluded spot where Leah and he could be alone.

On their walk to the riverside hideaway, they were free of all reality. They sat on a huge boulder on the riverbank and listened to sounds of the river flowing.

"Hertzka," Leah said lovingly, and she leaned over, putting her head on his shoulder and kissed him just below the ear.

Harry returned her kiss, and they made love by the river. It was the first time for both of them.

"We should get married right away," Harry said. "There's no reason to wait, with everything so crazy."

Leah could only agree. She felt love in Harry's arms and knew he would protect her.

"We will tell my father on Friday night," she said, "Although it might be better if you have your brother arrange it. My father respects Aria and he will feel better knowing that Aria gives us his blessing too."

Harry knew that Leah's father would welcome such an arrangement. The Hafts had plenty of food, and Leah would be safe and well fed.

Harry took Leah home, safely as he had promised. They stood in the doorway kissing, until Schmuel opened the door to investigate the noise.

Harry walked home carefully through the streets of the zone, staying in the gutter with other Jews. He stopped to talk to two friends when a horse and wagon passed. The horse relieved himself in front of them.

Before Harry could finish his conversation, four German soldiers grabbed the three young men for what they called cleaning duty. Without a word or even a look of distaste, Harry bent down and scooped up the horse dung with his bare hands. He refused to allow anything or anyone to spoil his engagement day.

On Wednesday, the day after Harry pledged himself to Leah,

Aria shook Harry awake in the very early morning. He hustled him outside to see what had happened overnight. There were big signs hanging throughout the Jewish zone. A proclamation commanded all men from the age of sixteen to fifty to report to the fire brigade building for registration by 11:00 A.M. that very day.

The fire brigade headquarters was in the center of town. It was a multipurpose, two-story structure with a large five-story tower on its east end. At the base of the tower was the main entrance that opened into a large meeting hall. The second floor of the building housed the cinema, where as a young boy Harry would sneak into many a show.

Aria and Harry stood outside reading the sign over and over.

"What do you think they're registering us for?"

Harry shrugged his shoulders and answered, "Maybe for work?"

"At least you are not sixteen yet."

True enough. It was June, a month shy of Harry's birthday.

Aria continued, "But I will have to register. Come back inside. Let's eat something and think."

The brothers sat down at the table and shared some bread and cheese. Harry knew this was the right time to tell Aria about Leah.

"I know you are concerned about this registration, but I have some good news. And I need your help."

"Hertzka, what now?" Aria was pulled out of his thoughts to hear more trouble from his brother.

"Leah and I are in love. Yesterday, we decided to marry."

Aria interrupted, "And what do you need me for?"

"She is going to tell her father on Friday, and I will need you to go see Meir to make the arrangements."

Harry expected some form of resistance from Aria, but there

was none. Aria recognized the intensity on his brother's face. He surprised Harry with his reply: "Why would any lovers wait, with everything going on? Meir Pablanski is a good man, and a good friend to me. You are lucky. You have my blessing. And Harry, she is a pretty girl. How could such a nice girl from such a good family choose a goon like you?"

Aria raised his cup, holding what was left of yesterday's warmed-over coffee. "I will do it for you," he said.

Harry never felt closer to his brother.

"Let me be the one to tell Mom the good news when she wakes up. It will give her some happiness before she sees the proclamation," Harry said.

"Yes, good idea. Meanwhile Hertzka, I have much to do today. I think I will get the registration over with early. If I go now, it won't take long, and I'll be back by lunchtime."

Aria put a small piece of cheese in his pocket and headed out to the firehouse, while Harry stayed home daydreaming of Leah.

When Hynda got up, Harry shared his good news with her. At first, she was not overjoyed. After all, Harry was her baby, and she was reluctant to let him go. Then she remembered that ten years before, Rosa and Peretz Kolton had offered to take young Harry with them to Russia, and she had refused. With events in Belchatow getting worse all the time, sometimes she regretted that decision. She could not interfere again in Harry's life.

By late afternoon, Aria had not returned. Hynda started to worry, and she sent Harry out to find out what had happened.

Harry approached several Jewish men talking across the street.

"Did you register?" Harry asked each one.

"Meshugener!" one replied. "You're crazy."

"We are not so stupid," said another.

"What are you talking about? asked Harry.

"Haven't you heard? Not one Jew who went to register has come back."

Harry decided to go to the firehouse to see for himself.

As he approached the firehouse, Harry saw a long, single line of perhaps two hundred townspeople surrounded by several dozen soldiers. The line was orderly and well supervised. It stretched from the building's main entrance out into the square. The only activity appeared to be at the front door to the building. The line bunched up to encircle a small wooden desk, where a German army captain, holding a large notebook, sat recording the names of the men before they were sent through the double entrance doors.

The captain was so busy that he didn't seem to see Harry nudge past the soldiers to a spot behind him. As a new registrant entered, Harry grabbed the door and called out his brother's name.

"Hey, Aria, Aria! Aria Haft, come to the door."

Inside, several of Aria's friends motioned for Harry to wait. Harry held the door for the next two Jews while his friends went looking for Aria. Before long, Aria stood facing Harry from inside the door. Another new detainee walked between them as Harry frantically asked, "What are you still doing here?"

Aria put his hand to his mouth, motioning for Harry to be quieter.

Aria whispered, "We were told we cannot leave. They have our names and addresses, and it will only mean great harm to you and Mother if I disobey."

"You have to get out of here," Harry begged.

"The word is that we're being taken somewhere tonight. We

think it's to work, but no one knows for sure. You're the one who must leave, *now*. Take care of Mom and keep doing business."

"No! No! Watch me. I'll get their attention, and you run. Please Aria, you must!"

Instinctively, Harry turned around and walked over to the captain sitting at the desk. He started to play drunk, fell over once, and was able to engage him in his tomfoolery. The soldiers closest to the table started laughing, and it seemed for a moment that Harry was successful in distracting them. Aria quickly seized the opportunity to run out the door and around the corner.

Harry's eyes followed Aria. Unfortunately, that was enough to tip off the captain. The moment of levity was over, and now the captain and his soldiers realized they had been had. The Germans had been caught off guard and had not given chase.

The clowning was over. The captain now stood before Harry and started screaming. "Where is he? Where did he go?"

A soldier grabbed Harry by the shirt and started to shake him.

"We lost one," the captain grunted. With that, the soldier who had been tricked started getting rough with Harry.

He yelled, "Where did he go? You are going to tell us."

A second soldier held onto Harry's other side. When Harry did not answer, the two soldiers dragged him to the opening of the doors. Before he could answer, they jammed his hand in the crack between the doors and slammed them shut.

Harry screamed out in pain, and his legs buckled.

"How would I know where he went?" he fumbled to say something.

"You know where he is, Jew! Now tell us!"

Harry didn't speak. With that, they grabbed his other hand, shoved it in between the doors, and slammed them.

Again Harry screamed out in pain, but he wouldn't talk. He refused to name his brother even though he knew half his fingers were broken.

The captain interrupted his men. "Enough. We are missing one, so he will do."

Harry was pushed inside to take his brother's place.

About four hundred men were stuffed into the main hall of the firehouse by nightfall, with plenty of soldiers outside to make sure they stayed there.

Many Jewish families lined the street outside, looking for the men who had not come home. It was nearing the curfew for Jews, and tension filled the air. Then the transports arrived.

Fifteen or sixteen buses, along with a small convoy of trucks full of soldiers, pulled in front of the building. The soldiers got out of their vehicles, weapons in hand, and joined in with the soldiers already in front of the building to facilitate the loading of the buses.

Emerging from daylong captivity, the detainees searched the crowd for familiar faces. No one was given the opportunity to say goodbye, and every one of the men urgently wanted to get a message to a family member.

Harry searched in vain for his mother or Leah, but there was no one there. An older man in front of Harry tried to reach out to his family before he climbed on the bus, but he was struck in the head with a rifle butt for holding up the line. The soldiers were well trained, and the buses were boarded with little resistance.

Leaving by the dark of night, Harry left his life behind, and started a new existence. It was no longer a life, just drudgery without a calendar, where days and months would become meaningless, and with only one memory to hold onto: that of Leah.

The buses traveled through the night and part of the next day. Not one Jew on board knew where they were going. Soon it became clear when the buses stopped at Poznan.

Poznan was in western Poland, less than one hundred and fifty miles from Berlin. When the buses pulled in, there were many soldiers waiting for the prisoners to disembark.

The new arrivals were quickly organized into groups. The first thing the Germans looked for were Jews who would make good "Jewish cops," men whose job would be to enforce the German rules and regulations and police the other Jews. Harry was not surprised to see who eagerly lined up for the "force." The local Jewish criminals and bullies saw an opportunity to save their own skins.

There were barracks ready for the new arrivals, but no food or water. Harry and the others were exhausted from the trip and bedded down, ignoring their worry, hunger, and thirst.

The following morning, at daybreak, soldiers entered the barracks with a stern wakeup call. Anyone who did not move fast enough was struck with the butt of a rifle.

"Quick, quick," the soldiers shouted as they lined up the Jews outside.

A brand-new black automobile pulled up right in front of them, and a civilian in a suit and tie emerged from the vehicle.

He walked to the head of the line and began arbitrarily dividing the group. "Left," he would tell some. "Right," he would tell others.

He sealed men's fates with a simple hand gesture. Harry was sent to the left. The left group was ordered to march off behind several soldiers who led the way. Harry never saw the men in the right line again.

Harry's group walked some distance to a place called Poznan

Dempsen. It became clear that there was a distinct profile to the men who made the march. All of them were young and strong. They were led to a new set of barracks, but this time, before entering, the men were lined up in single file and given a spoon and a cup.

There were several inmates already in the barracks to greet them. These men were the cooks and the cops.

The cooks portioned out Harry's first meal of potatoes and water. It was just enough to keep the group of men alive. While they were eating, the cops went over the rules of the barracks. The group was informed that they would be working for the German company Haman. They were told how they were expected to behave in order to stay alive.

Harry was not intimidated. He knew most of the Jewish cops as petty thieves from Belchatow.

"Hertzka Haft," a Jewish cop called out.

Harry knew this one well, and he apparently wanted to talk to him. Harry suspected the cop might be holding a grudge against someone in his family as he approached. Before the cop could speak, Harry said in a soft but firm voice only for his ears, "Now you be careful. Behave yourself when it comes to me. Don't you ever lift your arm against me or I'll break it."

Harry turned and walked away, feeling sure he had conveyed his message. This was Harry's way of introducing himself to life in a slave labor camp.

Lost Hope

THE NEXT MORNING the cops woke the men up early. It was to be their first day of work, and they were quickly dressed and assembled in front of the barracks. The SS officer took a count, found no one missing, and marched the group a short distance to the railroad yards. There the contingent was broken into smaller work details, and Harry's group was assigned to do cement work for the construction of a building to house locomotives.

After several days, Harry realized they would be working in the same location each day. He decided to study the surroundings. He was in the middle of a huge train depot, a railroad yard with tracks converging and spreading in all directions. It was a busy center of activity for the organization and distribution of supplies.

Harry observed that several times during his work day the soldiers guarding the trains changed shifts. When they made this change, there would be ten or fifteen minutes when the railroad yard was left unguarded. The smoke and noise from the movement of the trains could provide a cloak and the air was full of the smell of opportunity, he thought.

Naparella was the foreman assigned to Harry's construction site. Naparella worked for Haman. He was not a soldier, and he would often remind his workers of that in an attempt to win their loyalty. He was a tall, handsome, slightly balding man in his late thirties. Naparella's dark blond hair was slicked back, and his ears turned red anytime he had to scream to correct a worker's mistake.

Harry went out of his way to be friendly to his boss.

Naparella took notice of the broken fingers on the young man's hands, and seemed sympathetic. "Your name is?" he asked Harry on the second workday.

"Hertzka . . . Hertzka Haft."

"And you are very young. How is it that you are here?"

Harry told Naparella about the registration, how he helped his brother escape, and how his fingers were broken.

Harry sensed that Naparella felt sorry for him, especially when his face turned sour and he said, "Ah. We live in some terrible times. Who are our friends? Our enemies? You know I have a brother too who has caused me plenty of trouble. He was living in Berlin with his wife and children. They arrested him because he is a German communist. Now he is in Dachau, while I work for the fatherland. You know Dachau?"

"No."

"It's a terrible, terrible prison . . . best we not talk too much about it."

Harry was feeling close to Naparella. He was at ease in his presence. He didn't consider him a threat. They had made a personal connection, and Harry felt it was right to take a bold step further.

"You know, Mr. Naparella, I see that there are a number of trains coming in and going out." Harry said casually to feel him out.

"Yes, supplies pass through this junction for all the troops in Poland."

Then Harry asked a direct question: "Do you have any trouble getting stuff on or off the trains?" He tried not to appear too interested as he put out the bait.

Naparella answered, "No," and he put his hand on Harry's shoulder and looked directly in his eyes. "We are not allowed to go near the trains, and you can never leave the area where you work." Then he winked twice.

The workday ended, and Harry marched back to the barracks with his entire group. After the count, they were given their portion of potatoes and water and went to bed.

Harry was kept awake with his thoughts that night.

What did the wink mean? he wondered. Did it mean that if he got the chance, he should go down to the trains? Would he be able to hide on one? Would he be able to leave this place?

For just a moment, he imagined taking the train far away, back to Belchatow, and Leah. Then he fell asleep.

The next morning came soon enough. Harry arrived with his group to find Naparella in a very good mood. For the first time, Naparella gave out the day's instructions, but left out orders for Harry. He was made Naparella's assistant, and no one cared as they trudged off to start mixing cement. Harry knew immediately that Naparella expected him to watch the railyard and make a move when the guards changed shifts.

Harry made his way easily to the middle of a large freight train and crouched underneath a sealed boxcar. He picked up a piece of scrap metal and used it to pry open the lock. Then he slid open the door just enough to see what good fortune lay inside. The boxcar was full of tobacco products. He quickly chose to take a case of cigars rather than cigarettes. He pulled the door shut, secured the lock, and concealed the case as he walked back to the construction site.

In short order, Harry broke open the case and stuffed a box of cigars in his shirt. At the site, he hid the rest of the case in the foundation of the building and covered his treasure with debris.

He walked up to Naparella and motioned for him to come over to the side of the building. When they were out of the eyes and ears of the others, Harry pulled out the box of cigars and handed it to him.

"Can you use it?" asked Harry.

Naparella's eyes opened wide and a big smile crossed his face. "Sure, I can use it." And he put one arm around Harry in an embrace.

Harry saw that Naparella was tickled out of his mind. He was elated. He thought, "I have just bought my man, and he may be the one to help me."

"I have many more like that one," Harry whispered.

At the end of the work day, all of the other workers were marched back to camp. Naparella told the other foremen and the soldiers that he had more work for Harry in town. No one questioned Naparella's word.

In front of the others, he ordered Harry to follow him, and they walked in the direction of the hidden stash. When it was safe, Harry retrieved the case of cigars from its hiding place. Naparella opened the trunk of his car, and Harry put the case inside. He got into the front seat next to Naparella for the short ride to town.

Harry had no idea where they were going. In the heart of Poznan, Naparella pulled the car in front of a small white house and stopped. He motioned Harry to follow as he got out and took several boxes of cigars out of the case. He handed them to Harry to carry up the front stairs. The door to the house was open and they walked right in.

"Rini," called Naparella, and Rini appeared.

Rini was short and slender, a dark-haired Polish beauty with dazzling eyes and a warm smile. She was not shy about showing Naparella her affection, and they kissed for several moments in front of Harry.

"These are for you," Naparella motioned for Harry to put the boxes of cigars on the living room couch.

"Sit my man down in the kitchen with some food, and then bring me a drink. Better hurry, I still have some work to do, and I have to get him back to the camp."

Rini took Harry to the kitchen and placed some sausages and bread on the table. She poured him a glass of milk before she returned to the living room with a bottle of schnapps.

Harry tore into the meal and thought about escaping, but he was quickly distracted by the sounds of lovemaking in the other room. He felt the yearnings of his sixteen-year-old body, and he continued to eat. In about twenty minutes, Naparella returned fully dressed, but with uncombed hair.

"All right. We have more business to do." He said, kissing Rini goodbye and ushering Harry out the door.

They drove to another part of town where the same routine was repeated.

As it turned out, Naparella had three different Polish girl-friends in separate sections of Poznan, and a German wife with two children back home in Berlin.

Naparella told Harry that the girls would sell or trade the cigars for money or other goods. Each girl received her share of the bounty, and at each house Harry would be left in the kitchen with food while Naparella was entertained.

Harry would be alone in the kitchen, free and unsupervised.

But Poznan was a town where more and more citizens were becoming Nazis, and Harry knew he was safer in Naparella's care than out on the streets.

Harry's daily life in Poznan now consisted of stealing for Naparella in exchange for food and some protection.

Each day, Naparella saw to it that Harry was excused from his group's work detail. Harry was allowed to pick and choose a time to hit the trains. He became very good at it and was able to steal something every day. Clothing, sugar, coffee, tobacco, and all sorts of canned goods were at his disposal when the Germans were not watching the railroad cars. It was not long before Harry was able to make several runs a day.

Naparella didn't chance seeing his girlfriends every day, so he managed to get Harry a pushcart. Harry would steal in the morning and load the pushcart. Naparella affixed a Nazi flag on the far right corner of the wagon, and the goods were always covered with a blue plastic sheet.

Harry was never stopped when pushing the wagon the few short miles into town. He would make deliveries to each of Naparella's women. It thrilled him to pass SS men along the route who never looked twice to see what he was doing. As he passed them, he would feel his heart pounding, not from fear of being caught but from the thrill of stealing from the Germans.

Of Naparella's three girlfriends, Rini's house was always Harry's first stop. She was his favorite, and he always left her the largest share. Unlike the other girls, Rini treated Harry like a human being. She would allow him to rest on the living room couch, and she would serve him her best food and drink. Harry was very attracted to her and had to restrain himself desperately from displaying it.

While Harry would eat, Rini would sit and talk with him in the kitchen. She asked Harry questions about his home and family, and Harry could see pity and sadness for him as he recounted the story of how he came to Poznan.

Then one day, during one of their conversations, Rini asked a question that pained Harry greatly. "Hertzka, do you have a girlfriend back in Belchatow?"

"Yes," Harry said sadly and he put down his fork and stared at the floor, at her shoes.

Harry brought his head back up slowly, and he could not resist a look at her legs at the bottom of her skirt, just below her knees.

"What is her name?" Rini asked.

"Leah. We were planning to get married. I was about to ask her father to bless our engagement when I was sent here."

Harry went on to tell her the whole story, from the fight when he punched her father's teeth out, to proposing marriage by the river, and especially about not having a chance to say good-bye.

Rini touched his hand with understanding.

"Hertzka, I can help you."

"How?"

"I will write letters for you."

Even when Harry was still in Belchatow, mail service to Jews was unreliable.

"Rini, Jews cannot get mail, but I might have a way."

"Tell me. What is it?"

"Leah had a Polish girlfriend before all the trouble began. She lived on my street, and we were also acquaintances. Maybe if we write to her, she will deliver a letter to Leah and to my family. Her name is Zosha Kubiak, and I know her address."

Rini kept her word. She wrote to Zosha, and sure enough, a

note came back from Harry's brother and mother, and a sealed letter from Leah. So began a monthly ritual that continued as long as Harry made deliveries.

Harry received two love letters from Leah, the contents of which he could not bear to share with Rini. Leah's life in the Jewish sector was getting more difficult, and her father was gravely ill with typhus. Aria was still smuggling and doing well, and he made a promise to Harry to take care of Leah for him.

Harry knew he could confide in Naparella and told him of Rini's letter writing.

Naparella was surprised, but he recognized an opportunity. He told Harry to contact Aria about the possibility of buying dollars or gold with his German money. Aria wrote back that he could make a connection.

Naparella made arrangements for Harry to accompany him on the trip to Belchatow to make the buy, and he promised that Harry could see Leah and his family.

Harry was returning to Belchatow just as he had dreamed.

It was an all-day drive by car to reach Belchatow, made longer by countless stops at the German checkpoints along the road. Naparella carried impeccable identification for his passenger, and his black sedan waving the Nazi flag passed through most inspections with little delay.

They arrived in Belchatow in the early evening and drove straight to the Jewish sector. Naparella wanted to get Harry's visit with Leah out of the way so that they could concentrate on his business with Aria.

To Harry's surprise, the Jewish quarter was practically deserted. It looked as if everyone had been evacuated and only the sick remained, dying in the streets of starvation. This picture of despair had been kept from Harry in the letters, and now he saw for himself what had happened since he left. He felt alarmed as they approached Leah's apartment and found that it had been ransacked and nothing was left.

His worry now turned to fear for his family. Harry begged Naparella to drive to the outskirts of town, where his sister Brandel lived with her husband. From Aria's letters, he knew that Brandel was pregnant with her first child.

The sun was going down and it started getting colder and dark outside. The black sedan pulled into the street where Brandel lived. Two German trucks overloaded with people passed them on their left. A third truck was being filled with people right in front of Brandel's house. The Germans were cleaning out the neighborhood right in front of their eyes.

Harry watched from the car, paralyzed, as soldiers strongarmed his sister and her husband out of their house and onto the crowded truck. He heard pleading and screaming, and Brandel was crying out to someone as the truck started moving. The next thing Harry saw was a soldier coming out of the house with a baby in his arms, running toward the truck. The soldier tossed the newborn toward Brandel's outstretched arms, but he missed, and the baby crashed to the ground. Another soldier, without hesitation, pulled out a revolver, and shots rang out. The baby's body was left in the gutter.

It was on this day, at the age of sixteen, that Harry lost his belief in the existence of God. He was left with little hope that anyone in his family would survive.

Naparella knew it was too dangerous to stay in Belchatow another minute, so he turned the car around and drove all night back to Poznan.

Harry was immediately returned to his barrack once they were back in Poznan. The next morning he marched along side the other Jews to the worksite at the railyard. Outwardly nothing had changed. Naparella continued to have Harry steal from the trains. Naparella started seeing his girlfriends less frequently, so Harry walked with his pushcart to town more often.

Harry did not mind the long walk. He needed the solitude to think. His visit to Belchatow had changed him forever. His young mind was now in a dark place where numbness replaced feelings. A sense of the ruthlessness of his captors stayed with him; he felt his mortality at sixteen, a time when most boys think they will live forever.

It was clear to Rini that something was different. She saw it in Harry's face; his smile was gone. The conversation they once shared was now forced, and it eventually ended altogether. Harry never sat on the couch again. He confined himself to the kitchen where he was grateful to eat and rest.

Harry was angry, but also depressed and sorry for himself. He felt shame and guilt that he had not helped his sister. He felt responsible for the death of the baby, along with an overwhelming sense of captivity. He accepted that his relationship with Naparella was strictly business, an exchange of goods for food and protection.

Some months passed. Then in the middle of the night, without warning, the barracks were roused. Soldiers rounded the slave laborers onto buses by gunpoint. The buses took them to a train, where they were crammed into cattle cars.

The cattle cars had no windows, but there was ventilation through the wooden slats. It was the only relief for the men, jammed in tight without food or water. The train made many stops, but the doors never opened. There was unforgettable moaning and crying in the overcrowded space, and the stench of urine and feces was choking.

It was hard to tell, but the trip felt like it took a week.

When the doors finally opened, the men jumped out. As Harry jumped, he realized that a large number of men had died in the boxcar. He knew he was lucky that he had been so well fed at Poznan.

Harry hit the ground and immediately got to his feet. He was dizzy, and he squinted in the daylight. He watched as some men who jumped out of the boxcar were now not able to find the strength to stand. They were shot.

It seemed as if everyone around Harry was shot except for a few standing.

"Am I the living dead?" he thought.

They learned they were in Strzelin, another slave labor camp. Those who could walk were led by soldiers to barracks, where they were given enough bread and water to stay alive. Harry would now know hunger, for the first time, and he started losing weight rapidly. He looked for something to steal to help him survive.

The new inmates were allowed to sleep that night. Harry selected a spot to sleep next to a young man in his early twenties who looked strong enough to swap some protection with. For Harry, the young man had a comfortable familiarity, as though they had met before.

"Hertzka," Harry introduced himself.

"Schlemek Podrowski," the young man put out his hand.

They shook hands.

"Schlemek, if we are going to live, we will need to help each other."

"I could not agree more." said Schlemek.

"Then let's become brothers," and Harry found a sharp object.

Harry and Schlemek each pricked an arm, put blood on blood, and pledged to one another to give his life to save his new brother. The next morning, Harry and Schlemek marched with their group a few miles into the fields to begin clearing the land to lay railroad tracks.

The labor was hard, the steel tracks heavy, and the conditions were made worse by hunger and thirst. German soldiers, not civilians, were in charge. The soldiers were not as patient as the civilian foremen. They always expected the workers to move faster, and were brutal in their discipline. They looked for any reason to inflict pain, so, if you didn't walk straight, or talk right, or could not lift the heavy rail, you were shot. The brutality was so random that Harry felt lucky every day he survived.

Harry was in Stzelin for just over a month, and it felt like hell on earth. He could not even begin to imagine a worse hell until the night the transports came to take the inmates from Stzelin to Auschwitz.

The Beating

"TO YOUR GRAVE," the soldier answered, when Schlemek asked their destination as he boarded the truck.

Harry was right behind him. Not many knew about Auschwitz, and one soldier made sure to tell them that no one came back alive from it. The news made for a miserable journey.

Schlemek and Harry did not see any way out. You get on the trucks or your life ends in Stzelin. There is no choice.

The truck took them to the bus, and the bus took them to the train. Harry and Schlemek were determined to stay together, especially because this trip was Schlemek's first on a boxcar and he was terrified. Harry pushed others out of the way to stay near him and he reassured him, "Don't worry Schlemek. They always need people to work, and if we stay together, we will find a way."

Harry put his arm around Schlemek in the dark and closed his eyes to rest.

The journey to Auschwitz was not a long one, and everyone on board survived the ordeal. When the doors opened, the men got out of the boxcars and were told to stand in front of the train.

Soldiers walked through the crowd of new arrivals picking healthy and strong-looking people. Schlemek and Harry were chosen.

"You see, my friend," Harry told him, "we will work and we will eat. I will figure out a way to make our days bearable."

The soldiers directed the two of them to join another long line. Because the line was made up of other strong, healthy-looking people, they felt good about their chances. It turned out the line was for registration. When Harry got to the head of the line, he was asked his name, which was recorded into a log with a corresponding number. Next, that number, 144738, was tattooed in green ink on Harry's forearm. Schlemek, 144739, followed.

The tattooed prisoners were loaded onto trucks once again and driven a short distance to Birkenau. After disembarking, the new arrivals were lined up in single file. A commander went down the line, taking a good look at each person, and then he made his selection.

"Go left," he said, or "Go right."

Schlemek and Harry were sent to the left, hungry and filled with fear. A soft rain began to fall and they opened their mouths to the sky.

The group to the right was made to strip off all clothes. Schlemek and Harry watched with fear, and then envy, when the men were given a portion of bread, a piece of soap, and a towel and then marched in the direction of the showers. Harry and Schlemek could not know that those envied were marching off to be gassed.

It was not yet evening, but the sky was dark and full of rain clouds. Black smoke bellowing from several chimneys nearby contributed to the early darkness. The group remaining was marched into barracks, and given a small piece of bread and a drink of water.

Schlemek, Harry, and several other men were selected to start work right away, even before they could get a night's rest at Birkenau.

That first night would be the beginning of the toughest time Harry spent in the camps. The men were assigned to the crematorium, where wagons full of naked, freshly gassed men, women, and children were dumped at their feet. It was their job to toss the bodies into an oven. Harry tried not to look at the faces of the dead, but he could not help it. It took two men to toss an adult into the fire, but Harry was expected to handle the bodies of children on his own. Harry found himself feeling sorry for the first time that he was strong enough to work, and therefore, to remain alive. He felt a kinship with the dead people. He felt dead and alive at the same time. He could not help counting the number of bodies he helped burn. He lived with the smell of burning flesh and he could not rid himself of it, even later back at the barracks.

One day, Harry was reminded that he could still feel. A worker from his group found his own wife lying in the first pile of bodies that morning. He went crazy. This shy, ordinarily quiet man attacked the guard closest to them as though he no longer cared about himself. He was shot on the spot.

Harry and Schlemek were directed by the guards to throw his body into the fire. Harry grabbed the legs and Schlemek the shoulders, and just before they heaved forward, Harry caught sight of the man's face. His eyes were open; he was not dead. Next, they reached for the man's wife and threw her in beside him.

The vision of that man burning was too much for Harry to bear. The next day, when it came time to go to work in the crematorium, Harry refused to go. He broke down like a child. He could not do it anymore. He was ready for the consequences even if it meant it was time to die.

A German SS officer, with rank, stepped forward. "Give this man to me. I can use him," he said.

Harry was spared and found himself assigned to another job.

He no longer spent his days with the corpses. He was assigned to a group called the Sonderkommando. The belongings of all who came to Birkenau were thrown into a warehouse on the grounds of the camp. It was the job of the Sonderkommando to sift through the clothes looking for items of value, such as gold, jewelry, and currency.

For Harry, it was a tremendous relief to be away from the corpses. For the officer, Schneider, it was an opportunity.

Harry recognized that Schneider had saved his life, and he was determined to work hard for him. But Schneider had something else in mind.

Acknowledging the debt he owed Schneider, Harry said to him, "Anything you want me to do for you, I will do."

Schneider raised his eyebrows. "Anything?"

"Anything."

"How do I know I can trust you?"

"My life is in your hands."

"But can you keep secrets?"

"I would die before I told a secret," and Harry stuck out his right hand. "Do you see my hand? My broken fingers? They tried to make me talk even put my hand in a door but I never talked."

Schneider smiled. He thought for a moment. He then said to Harry, "You are going to stay alive here. I will see to that. I want to live after the war, and you will help me do that."

Harry believed Schneider. He already knew he was no ordinary soldier when he spared him. He had high rank. But Harry could not help wondering what the price was going to be for his protection.

Days passed without further discussion. Then one morning Schneider gave Harry a small empty whiskey bottle to use as a container. He walked Harry back to his barracks and saw to it that Harry found a place in his bedding to hide the container.

He then explained that Harry would forage through the discarded possessions for jewels. Every day Schneider would make sure that Harry was able to take back to the barracks two or three nice diamonds. When Harry crawled into his bunk, he would deposit the catch in the whiskey bottle. After several weeks, he had accumulated enough for the bottle to be half full.

One day, for whatever reason, a group of soldiers entered the barracks. One bunk was indistinguishable from another, but the soldiers went right to Harry's spot. One soldier poked his rifle in the bedding and pulled it from the tight ledge.

The bottle was exposed.

Harry was taken to the storage room where he was interrogated and beaten. The beating was severe, and the guards were able to get Harry to confess to stealing the diamonds. Despite the torture, Harry never mentioned Schneider.

Harry was then dragged out of the barracks and taken to a building that housed the Strafkommando. Here the prisoners were taken to be punished for breaking camp rules.

A prisoner sent to the Strafkommando might live perhaps another day or two before being killed. It was a place where the most horrible pain was inflicted, where the guards punched and kicked and beat their victims with rifles, clubs, and chains.

Harry endured a horrible beating. He was lying on the ground unable to move when he heard a familiar voice.

"This man is mine," Schneider commanded the guards. "I need this man, bring him to me."

The guards lifted the bloodied and battered Harry off the floor. Harry could not stand, so Schneider grabbed him under one arm and dragged him out of the building to a single truck sitting at the front gate. The truck was packed with Jews, and there was no room for Harry, so Schneider pulled a Jew off the transport and put Harry in his place.

Minutes later, the truck pulled away.

Harry was badly bruised and battered, but miraculously still alive. His strength returned with the knowledge that he made it through and had another opportunity to live. He felt a bulge in the pocket of his pants, and he traced his fingers around the shape of a bottle. Schneider had slipped a new bottle to Harry, but this time the bottle was full of whiskey. Harry drank half the bottle and traded the other half for a piece of bread, making the ride out of Birkenau more than bearable.

Jew Animal

HARRY HAD BARELY FINISHED his piece of bread when the truck pulled into the gates of a new camp just an hour down the road. Jaworzno was a working coal mine that served as another slave labor camp.

Harry was taken with the others to the barracks on a block that held nearly one thousand workers. Work in the coal mines was done in two shifts, and Harry was assigned to the night shift.

The mineshafts were not close, so a number of German soldiers and Jewish cops would march the workers to the job site and back. To control the large number of workers, the guards would line everyone up in five rows and cuff one leg of each prisoner to a long chain.

This was Harry's first experience on a chain gang. The Jewish cops and guards marched the group at a brisk pace on their five-mile journey to the mines each night. As a new arrival, Harry was unfamiliar with the routine, and because of his recent beatings, marching was difficult.

On his first day of work, as Harry was being shackled, he looked into the face of the Jewish cop locking him to the chain, and he knew the man's face. It was Mischa, a hoodlum from Belchatow. He was the type of guy who would profess to be your friend and then steal from you. Their eyes locked.

"Mischa, you scumbag. You're with them?"

"I have to live, you know," he replied, and he moved on to the next leg.

Then it was time for the cadence. Mischa joined in. "Left, right, left, right . . ." Harry felt uncoordinated and found it difficult to follow. His clumsiness caused the other men to lose balance, and they were forced to stop and rearrange the tangled chains.

Mischa spotted the disruption and ran toward Harry. With the guards watching, he planted himself directly next to Harry's face and screamed "Left, right . . ." in his ears. He kicked Harry and hit him hard in the back with a baton.

Harry made it to the mineshaft for his first day's work, but he was hurt.

From that day on, Mischa took a personal interest in Harry. With the guards' permission, he would beat Harry daily on the way to the mineshaft. Those first days of work in the Jaworzno coal mine began with a beating from his Jewish neighbor.

There were days when Harry would beg Mischa to leave him alone. Mischa seemed to enjoy showing the guards how he kicked and struck Harry with his stick.

Harry worked with a group of men whose job was to carry explosives into the mountains where it would then be discharged. Following this, they would pick up and load the dislodged coal onto wagons. The men in charge of the work in the coal mines were private Polish citizens under the direction of soldiers. This was slave labor for the Poles as well as the prisoners, and it made these men hate both the prisoners they sweated with and the soldiers standing over them. The prisoners were treated harshly by the Poles, who blamed them for their predicament but could not retaliate against the soldiers.

Six days a week, with rest on Sundays, they toiled in the mines for months on end. With their bare hands, they loaded the coal onto the wagons. Despite being given water to wash with at the end of the shift, Harry was unable to remove all of the grime. His hands were now as dark and dirty as his miserable existence.

Quite unexpectedly, while loading a wagon one day, Harry spotted Schneider, wearing a uniform decorated with a high rank, walking toward him. Harry was speechless as Schneider stood before him and instructed him to follow him away from the others. Was this a dream? It felt as if God was in Harry's presence for the moment.

"Well, well. Don't you find it interesting that once we were stealing diamonds, and now we are mining coal?" Schneider spoke as though no time had passed.

Harry knew it was no dream when Schneider pulled from his pocket the little whiskey bottle and gave it to Harry to finish. That was real enough for Harry's throat.

"I'm not surprised to see you alive!"

Harry nodded and said "Thanks." He was beginning to learn that surviving was considered a compliment.

Schneider took some bread and sausage out of his other pocket and handed it to Harry. While Harry ate, Schneider confided to him that the war was no longer going as well for the Germans as a year before. Then he took off his jacket, rolled up his sleeve and said, "Come closer, I want to show you something."

Harry got closer. Schneider lifted his arm.

"I too have numbers. Do you see them?"

Harry looked at the numbers on his underarm.

"What are they for?" he asked.

"This is to identify me. Should I be killed, they would know who I was. It has my blood type, too."

He continued, "See what happens when you reach my rank?" He looked at Harry's confused face. "But why am I showing you? Well, my problems will come after the war. The Russians and the Americans will come looking for the ranking officers, and when I am captured, my tattoo will give them my identity, and I will have to pay for all this."

"I don't understand what this has to do with me," Harry spoke up.

"When word spreads about all of this, all of you, they will hunt us down." Harry still wondered why Schneider was being so open with him. "So I came to find you. By keeping you alive, you will owe me. You are my witness that I was not like the rest." Schneider rolled down his sleeve, buttoned it, and put his jacket back on. "Will you be my witness?" he asked Harry.

"Of course."

"Good. Then I will do what I can for you. Finish eating. I will see you tomorrow."

The next day Schneider kept his word and showed up around midnight. He gave Harry whiskey and chocolate to bribe the Polish foreman. With this, Harry was able to buy an easier assignment at the mine. He was now in the good graces of the ill-tempered foreman who swung his stick at others.

Harry loved the sausages that Schneider brought. He soon grew fat from them. To be fat in a slave labor camp is quite a spectacle, but because Harry was a tough guy, no one dared mess with him.

It was not long before word spread through the camp that

Harry was a protected man. When Mischa found out that a high-ranking officer was looking out for Harry Haft, he backed off. Harry was now able to march to the mines in his chains without being kicked or hit, but he swore he would never forget the pleasure Mischa took in his cruelty toward him.

Although Harry enjoyed an uncommon immunity from the crueler aspects of camp life, having a guardian angel did not excuse him from the dangerous work he had to perform in the coal mines at night.

One night Harry stood too close to a cave wall packed with dynamite. He knew how to shield his body from the explosion, but this time when the charge was detonated, shards of jagged rock from the blast struck Harry in the leg. Harry knew at impact that his foot was broken.

As he was carried out of the mine, the pain in his leg was accompanied with the grim knowledge that this injury could send him straight to Auschwitz. When a Jewish worker was hurt on the job, he was taken to the camp hospital, not to see the German doctors but to wait for the next transport to Auschwitz.

Harry was placed in a coal wagon by his fellow workers. The sun was just coming up as he was wheeled into the hospital. The men placed him on the floor of a ward full of feverish Jews moaning in their bedding. Hours passed and he knew unless he could get up and walk back to camp, he would be sent away with the other patients.

About midday, Schneider entered the ward accompanied by the head doctor.

"That man in the corner," he pointed to Harry, "He is my personal worker. Don't you dare put him on the transport, or you will deal with me."

The message was clear. The doctor motioned to his staff to put Harry on a bed. "No," the doctor responded, "As you wish. I will take a look at him."

They walked over to Harry. While the doctor prepared to examine the leg, Schneider pulled a bottle of whiskey from his pocket and poured some into a cup near the bed. He handed the cup to Harry.

"The leg is broken. He will have to be in a cast for six weeks," said the doctor. "What will I do with him for six weeks?"

"Give him a job in the hospital."

"What job?"

"You will make him a cleanup man."

"Fine," said the doctor.

The doctor kept his word and treated the leg. Harry moved into the hospital for the duration of his recovery. He remained a janitor for what turned out to be several weeks longer than six weeks, until the day he could walk with all his strength back to the barracks to resume work in the coal mines.

Returning to the barracks was a welcome change for Harry. In the hospital, the sick and injured were doomed. Harry could not bear the begging of the men he could not help, so he shut out the crying, and did not talk to anyone during the day. It was only at night when the cold was unbearable that he was able to secretly provide an extra blanket or rag to one or two of the sick.

Back at work, Schneider would come every night to Harry's jobsite about midnight. He would bring Harry bread, chocolate, meat, and, of course, a taste from his bottle of whiskey. Once again, Harry used some of the rations to secure the good will of the Polish foreman who took him back on the shift as before. But mainly he consumed the food, for he knew that tomorrow might bring hunger again. He quickly gained weight and became known as the only fat Jew in Jaworzno.

Early one morning, Harry was returning from the night shift when he met a friend from another work detail who had waited up all night to greet him with news.

"Hertzka, your brother Peretz has just come in from Lodz."

"Where is he?"

"Block 5."

"Thank you Yankel," and he went back to line up with the other workers for the nightly count.

Following the count, he headed out to Block 5. The Jewish cops in his barracks knew he was protected and allowed him to walk free. When Harry got to Block 5, he walked up and down the row of barracks yelling out, "Peretz Haft!"

He looked around and waited. A young man came out of the barracks and walked toward him.

"Yes, sir," said Peretz, and he put his hand to his forehead and saluted Harry.

Harry was so fat that Peretz did not recognize him.

"Peretz, it's me, Hertzka don't you know me?"

They embraced. Peretz was a small man, at least six inches shorter than Harry, and he could not have weighed more than one hundred pounds that day. Peretz did not look healthy. Harry could see that the train ride from Lodz had been a rough one for his brother, and he knew it was his responsibility to keep him alive.

Harry had brought some bread in his pocket and gave it to Peretz. He watched him chew the bread slowly, tasting every morsel before swallowing.

At midnight, when Schneider came as usual, Harry asked him to arrange for Peretz to work near him in the mines. Schneider made sure that weak Peretz was assigned an easier job of connecting the coal wagons to the trains.

Harry shared the extra food from Schneider with Peretz, and soon Peretz grew healthier and stronger.

Time passed, and then another crisis. Peretz was connecting two wagons together when one slipped and the cart rolled over his foot, trapping it under the wheel. His foot was broken. He was wheeled to the camp hospital to await the next transport to Auschwitz.

When Harry learned of his brother's misfortune, he knew he had to get to the hospital by 4:00 to intercept the transport. Harry was able to get out of his barracks while everyone slept at about 2:00 in the afternoon.

He didn't know how to reach Schneider, so he went directly to the doctor in charge. Luckily, it was the same doctor he had encountered before.

"Doctor, my brother was brought in yesterday. The man with the broken foot?"

"You are back?"

"Doctor, my brother is in here, and you are going to heal him just like you healed me, and you will put him to work as the clean up man until he can return to the mines."

The doctor did not say a word but his face reflected his surprise at Harry's firm tone of voice.

Harry went on, "If you need to talk with Schneider, I will go get him."

The doctor shook his head no and let out a muted laugh at Harry's arrogance, and then he said, "Show me your brother. I will treat him. But mind how you speak to me in the future. Just remember you're a Jew."

Harry was relieved and did not want to disrespect the doctor. "Yes, doctor," Harry promised.

One Sunday afternoon, Schneider visited Harry at his barracks. "Come outside, let's talk," he said. "I have some exciting news for you."

Harry could not imagine what that might mean. Was the war over?

Schneider left him to his imagination for a moment, and led him to the side of the barracks. He pulled out his whiskey as usual, but this time he offered Harry the first slug from the bottle. Harry could not resist a good swallow of the amber liquid.

"Now you are a big, strong Jew, my friend, and I am going to make you an entertainer."

"A what?" Harry asked.

"An entertainer. You are going to entertain my friends the other officers and soldiers. You are going to be a boxer, and on Sundays you will fight. Next Sunday, we will hold boxing matches in the street in front of the officer's quarters."

Harry owed Schneider his life, so he trusted him.

"All right. Whatever you say."

From then on, Schneider arranged for Harry to be given light duty at the mines, and they talked about the upcoming fights at their midnight rendezvous.

Schneider explained to Harry that his challengers would be other prisoners who would fight to earn extra rations. The fights were to be bare knuckle fights, although Harry could choose to wear a pair of Schneider's winter gloves. He went on to describe that the fights would end when one fighter was unable to continue.

That first Sunday, at 3:00, Schneider arrived at Harry's barrack to escort him to the SS camp. Harry didn't feel scared or nervous.

By now he was numb to the things he had to do to survive. It was enough that he knew he owed Schneider, and he didn't think beyond that. Schneider pulled out a pair of gloves from his jacket and gave them to Harry.

"You would be smart to use these to protect your hands. You will be having three or four fights."

Harry took his advice and put them on. The gloves were ordinary leather winter gloves, used and well broken in.

A makeshift ring was set up in the street in front of the SS quarters. Four wooden posts were driven into the ground, with a rope strung through holes to form a square. A crowd was quickly gathering. Chairs were placed all around the ring, and soon a theater atmosphere, with three or four rows deep was created. Soldiers stood around, eating, drinking, talking, and laughing, and music was provided by several Jewish prisoners playing string instruments.

Harry entered the ring and Schneider pulled up a chair to act as his corner man. Another soldier brought over a bucket of water, and a towel, which Schneider placed at his feet. He joined the party by taking a large swig from his whiskey bottle.

A soldier, acting as referee in the center of the ring, told Harry to remove his shirt and toss it to him. The soldier approached Harry and felt Harry's gloves to make sure he was not hiding anything inside.

The first opponent was brought into the ring. Harry was shocked by his appearance. He saw before him a half-dead skeleton of a man. It became clear to him at that moment that there would be nothing fair about this match. Harry was eighteen years old, big and strong. Schneider had kept him well fed, not overworked or tortured. Harry looked across the ring and saw the fear on the face of his challenger, and he knew that this man had not volunteered. Harry remembered Schneider's words about how the fight would end when one man was unable to continue, and now he understood what that meant.

Harry looked at the soldiers watching the ring. There was an eerie sense of merriment in the crowd. They were waiting for the show. He was there to show these sick bastards a good time. It would be a sport to watch a Jew kill another Jew.

Just about everyone was seated when the soldier acting as the referee ordered, "Go."

Harry could see that his opponent was defenseless, and he hesitated. He could hear the soldiers screaming anti-Semitic curses at them. Harry knew what they were screaming for. They were cheering him on to kill the other Jew with his fists. He felt sure that they would shoot him if he refused. So he complied.

The first time Harry knocked the other man down; the referee had to pick him up. The second time Harry knocked him down, he was unconscious, and was carried away.

Harry returned to his corner where Schneider sat on his throne. Schneider offered Harry a sip of his whiskey as a reward, but he declined. The match had barely lasted five minutes.

Next came another half-dead challenger. Harry fought five Jews that first Sunday. With each successive fight, Harry learned how to "entertain" the SS officers. The more brutally Harry beat up a man, the wilder the crowd became. Harry learned how to play with a man before finishing him off. This behavior energized the crowd to an inhuman pitch.

Of course, Harry knew that the men he knocked unconscious were not dead when they were dragged out of the ring. He visualized them being taken to the camp hospital to wait for the Monday transport to Auschwitz. Schneider actually tried to quiet Harry's guilt after the bouts by telling him that these men were going to end up in Auschwitz anyway.

This charade became the new weekly routine. Every Sunday, Harry was an entertainer, fighting half a dozen half-dead challengers. Harry became well known to the SS officers and was nicknamed "The Jew Animal" for his savagery. After each fight, Schneider was happy to escort Harry back to his quarters so he could tell him how grateful he was for the day's entertainment.

The "entertainment" went on for several months. By this time, Harry had fought seventy-five matches as the "Jew Animal" of Jaworzno, and he remembered few of the faces of the men he fought.

Then one Sunday morning, Schneider appeared earlier than usual to escort Harry to the officer's camp. He was happier than usual too, and more excited this day. Harry could sense that something was different this day and he asked,

"What's going on today?"

"Come. I'll tell you as we walk."

They walked out of the barracks and into the road. Schneider said, "I don't mean to alarm you with what I am going to tell you, but some generals from Berlin are coming to watch today."

"So?"

"Well, you have gotten yourself quite a reputation, and it has aroused their interest. The word is that there isn't a Jew in Poland who can defeat you. And I of course agree with that."

"And?"

"And so the generals have brought their own fighter today. I am told he is also undefeated, and he is not from Poland. The soldiers who have seen you fight have put up their own money to back you. I myself have put up money."

Harry did not fully understand Schneider's message. "Everyone here is counting on me?" he asked.

"Yes. And if you lose, no guard in this camp will be happy with you."

Now Harry understood.

"Don't worry. Your money is safe. I won't lose."

Schneider was not as confident. He knew a little more about Harry's opponent that he was willing to tell Harry on the walk.

There was a huge crowd in the SS camp this day. For the first time, there were nicely dressed women cavorting with the soldiers. The ring was rigged more professionally, with three ropes ringing the posts instead of one. There were extra rows of chairs surrounding the ring as if to accommodate a bigger crowd, and now there was a small orchestra of at least a dozen Jews playing music.

Harry climbed into the ring amid thunderous cheers from the guards of the camp. Schneider took his position in Harry's corner with the usual bucket and towel. As Harry began putting his gloves on, Schneider stopped him.

"There will be only one fight today, for all the money. Do not use the gloves. Your opponent will not use gloves."

With that, he pulled his bottle of whiskey from his pocket, turned his face away from Harry, and put it to his lips and swallowed several times.

Harry leaned against the corner post of the ring and waited. The onlookers were growing impatient and began stamping their feet and making noise any way they could.

An unfamiliar referee climbed into the center of the ring. He made several announcements, gave a long welcome speech that was barely heard above the noise, and then called the crowd's attention to the two generals seated in the second row. They were not hard to spot, with the cigars in their mouths, each draped with a beautiful girl holding a large liquor bottle. The generals stood and waved to the crowd.

Harry looked over at Schneider, who was now finishing his bottle of whiskey.

"We have plenty riding on you, Hertzka." This was the first time Schneider had called him by his first name.

It was time for his opponent to enter the ring. Two soldiers escorted the generals' man down the path leading up the stairs. Harry's opponent was a French Jew about ten years older than he. He was very tall, about six-three to Harry's five-nine, obviously well nourished, and he had long, muscular arms.

The referee introduced the rivals to the eager and impatient crowd. Harry was introduced as the undefeated and savage "Jew Animal of Jaworzno." His opponent was proclaimed to be the former heavyweight champion of France. The referee motioned for the fighters to come to the center of the ring for instructions.

"Rounds will be three minutes, with one-minute rests. I am here to see that you fight fairly. Box, do not turn this into a street fight. We will use a bell to start and stop the rounds. Do you understand?"

"How many rounds?" asked Harry.

"Until there is a winner," was the answer. "Go back to your corner and wait for the bell."

The bell rang.

The Frenchman was a slick mover, and Harry found it tough to land a punch on him. Harry was a flat-footed, toe-to-toe puncher, and it was the first time he had fought someone who wanted to box and run. Harry decided early on to try and fight smart. He knew the rounds would seem endless, and he decided not to waste too much energy chasing the Frenchman around the ring.

Harry stood in the center of the ring. "Fight like a man, Frenchy," he called out and motioned him to come closer. The crowd began booing the French fighter for not coming to meet Harry in the center of the ring to fight. The booing was incessant. Harry stood in the center ready to fight, and the Frenchman had to know that the booing was making him look like a coward, so he was forced to come in and take his best shots.

A skilled and experienced boxer, the Frenchman peppered Harry's face with hard jabs. After four or five rounds, Harry's eyes were cut and bleeding. Schneider tended to Harry's wounds between rounds with his bucket of water and towel.

As the rounds went on, Harry's bleeding became so profuse that he could barely see. His strength had not diminished, but he was hampered by his diminished sight. His survival was now not assured, and his mind snapped.

Harry lured the Frenchman into a corner of the ring, turned, and trapped him. With all the fury and rage inside him, Harry went wild, throwing blow after blow.

Slowly, the Frenchman was toppled like a giant tree being chopped down in the forest. Harry continued to pound at him as he went down, stopping only when the Frenchman's face was flush with the bottom of the ring.

Harry stood above waiting for him to get up; his blood ran down his face onto his adversary. The generals and their guests from Berlin stood and screamed at their man to get up. But he could not; he lay unconscious.

Schneider jumped into the ring to raise Harry's arms in victory. The camp's guards cheered wildly.

Harry watched the Frenchman being dragged from the ring and taken out of sight. Amid the noise and revelry of the crowd, Harry thought he heard two gunshots, but he was not certain. His ears were still ringing from the beating he took.

Harry never saw or heard of the French boxer again.

The Cannibals

HARRY'S REWARD for winning the fight was some time off from work in the mines, and he took advantage of it. It was during this time of rest from his battle that word spread through the camp that the Russians were closing in. It was hard to ignore the sounds of bombing raids that grew louder every night, and the guards were beginning to show their anxiety.

One night the bombing was intense and unending. The prisoners greeted the sounds with hope until the German army mobilized and roused the inmates in the dead of the night. The men were lined up to evacuate the camp.

Several thousand Jews were set to march. Harry grabbed Peretz and made his way to the front of the line, as his experience had taught that it was often safer there.

Schneider saw Harry and Peretz in the front, and he walked the two of them over to several officers to remind them that they were his personal workers and that no harm should come to them.

The assault on the camp began as thousands of inmates poured out of the front gates of Yavorshno. Harry wondered why the Germans would go to the trouble of moving them when they could have easily been killed by Russian bombs.

The exodus was at a fast pace, and those who were too slow,

too tired, or sick were shot and left like a trail of sticks along the road.

They walked for weeks, all day, stopping at night to rest. The marchers were able to find some food along the way, and the guards directed them to nearby farms where they would sleep in abandoned barns.

One cold night, Harry was led to a barn with very deep hay. A brilliant thought occurred to him. At daylight, when it would be time to resume the march, he would hide in the stacks of hay. Unfortunately, Harry was not the only one with this idea, and the Germans were not fooled. They went through the hay with bayonets and pitchforks to ferret out those in hiding. Men found hiding in the hay were shot on the spot, no questions asked.

Harry was stabbed with a pitchfork in his side and screamed out in pain. He was pulled out from the hay by a soldier who seemed to recognize him.

"The boxer. I've wounded the Animal," he told the others.

Other soldiers came over to confirm the find. They were all happy to see the boxer, and no one made too much of a fuss about his attempt to escape. They scolded him the way a mother would scold a child who spilled a drink. They even gave him a clean cloth to cover his wounds, and then escorted him to the front of the line to rejoin Peretz.

Out of several thousand Jews who left Jaworzno, only about two hundred made it to the intended destination, a train station. The soldiers loaded the survivors into a single boxcar, and slammed the doors shut. Peretz and Harry stayed together feeling like two brothers who were buried alive.

In the dark agony of the trip, Harry listened to the sounds of men dying, the moaning, the groaning, the crying and then the quiet. He was too weak to count the days spent on the train, and when the doors were opened, only thirty men were still alive.

Harry and Peretz helped each other to the ground. The remaining survivors were rewarded with a piece of bread and some water. It was not enough to ease the pains of hunger, but just enough to keep them standing. Harry sensed there might not be any more food for some time.

They were now in Flossenburg, in Germany, near the Czech border. Harry's instincts were right. Flossenburg was a disaster of a camp, with little food or water. There was no work to do and therefore there was little reason for the German soldiers to keep the prisoners alive. A rainy day was considered a lucky day because it provided water.

In Flossenburg, Harry and Peretz stayed huddled in their bunks day and night. They dared not move about. The extreme hunger forced them to conserve their energy.

In Flossenburg, the days were bad, but it was at night that the real terror in the barracks began. Harry and Peretz found themselves living in a nightmare worse than any they had experienced. The hopeless conditions pushed their fellow prisoners struggling for survival to abandon all semblance of humanity.

People cried out in the darkness in pain from being hungry, and the hunger drove them out of their minds. Some howled like wolves, and others were transformed into predators of the lowest order. If you were weak or sick, if you were alone, you could become their next prey.

Harry and Peretz took turns sleeping. One of them always remained awake, although there were times when neither could sleep because of the sounds of the atrocities being committed in the darkness.

Flossenburg pushed the boundaries of sanity beyond limit, to the unthinkable. The night killers in the Flossenburg barracks were other inmates who banded together to stave off death by hunger by eating human flesh.

Harry and Peretz never considered joining in, but they were consumed by the overwhelming guilt of watching the murders and doing nothing to stop them.

Just fifteen feet from their bunk, they bore witness to the horror. Three Russian Jews crept up on a new arrival who had fallen into a deep sleep following his harrowing journey to the new camp. He was alone, unprotected, and vulnerable.

Harry and Peretz were lying on their stomachs, huddled together, watching and not saying a word. The Russians used a piece of rope meant to hold up a pair of pants to strangle him to death. The man tried to fight but was overpowered, and in seconds his kicking and squirming ceased.

Harry and Peretz continued to watch, afraid to move. One of the Russians looked in their direction for a moment, but they feigned sleep. The killers then turned the man over and took his pants down. With makeshift knives, they cut into his ass and ripped off pieces of flesh. To Harry, it seemed like an eternity as they sat near him eating their kill. He could smell the blood.

A nightly ritual of terror began as Harry and Peretz would cling together in one bunk while some other emaciated soul was cannibalized after being strangled, suffocated, or, for those who put up a fight, stabbed through the heart with a crude homemade weapon.

As time passed and the starvation annihilated any remains of decency and sanity, cannibalism increased. Harry and Peretz knew they could not interfere with the murders. It wouldn't take much provocation for their deranged cellmates to turn their animal hunger on them as their next victims.

The following morning, the killers would throw the stinking torsos and body parts outside the barracks. Though the evidence was removed, this could not dispel the stench of blood throughout the sleeping quarters, and it served as a constant reminder of the horror that would begin again at nightfall.

It became impossible to fall asleep. The late night sounds of humans being sacrificed mingled with the bomb blasts getting closer each day and formed a frightening symphony that filled the ears and tortured the soul.

Within days, Flossenburg was being bombed. The Germans handed out bread to the detainees and loaded them into trucks. Harry knew it was a good sign that they were being fed, to be kept alive to work, and he and Peretz managed to board the same truck despite the confusion of the hasty departure.

The truck trip was a rough four-day journey back across Czechoslovakia and into Poland. Harry and Peretz had long ago finished their portion of bread when the trucks were unloaded at Rogoznica, a concentration camp the Germans called Gross-Rosen.

Surprisingly, they were met at Gross-Rosen with more bread and potato soup and some rest in their new barracks. The next day they were given yet another serving of bread and potato soup. When they were a bit stronger, they were told of work that would require them to report early in the morning at the front gate.

Harry made sure he was one of the first men at the gate before the sun rose. He smelled opportunity, and one day he got lucky.

The Germans needed a work detail of strong men to help unload trucks. Harry knew this job would put him close to something to steal, and he was right. The trucks that Harry unloaded contained tobacco.

Harry knew that he would be searched when he returned to the camp. He had been out on other jobs and was familiar with the search routine conducted by the guards at the gate. He knew that they were not going to let him smuggle in packs of cigarettes, and he also knew that if he were caught trying, the punishment would be death. That consequence, though never far away from his thoughts, did not replace the everyday struggle to survive, and so, despite the great risk, Harry filled his torn shoes with cigarettes.

He was cool when he approached the search line. The guard did not go near his shoes and let him enter the camp. For the next two weeks, he traded cigarettes for bread with the other prisoners, and he and Peretz regained their strength.

Gross-Rosen was evacuated shortly thereafter. Harry and Peretz soon found themselves back on a truck heading to the train. The brothers were now experienced boxcar travelers, and the two-day trip was tolerable because of the bread in their pockets from the tobacco trading.

The Escape

WHEN THE DOORS of the boxcar opened, Harry and Peretz were relieved that all the occupants had survived and were able to jump down with their own strength. Their destination turned out to be just outside Amberg, Germany, west of the Bohemian Forest, at the edge of a large airfield.

The men were taken to their barracks and given plenty of food and water. It was obvious to all that the Germans wanted the men strong for the work to come.

The next day, Harry, Peretz, and the others started work in the Krupp factory, cleaning airplanes and assisting repair crews. Harry worked with heavy equipment, and the airplane mechanics who oversaw the work were impressed with his strength.

Only a small number of troops guarded the labor in the Krupp factory, and as far as Harry was concerned, he experienced a sense of freedom because he was rarely supervised.

For Harry and Peretz, the best thing about this work was the fact that the runway was surrounded on all sides by potato fields. And the guards didn't care if the workers went in the fields on breaks to gather potatoes to bring back to the factory.

When the sun went down, the workers piled wood in the middle of the airfield and started a fire. One night, the mood was festive, and Harry, Peretz, and half a dozen others had a potato roasting to celebrate the rumors of an American invasion. The German guards stood by and watched the festivities around the bonfire, and some even shared some potatoes.

Suddenly, without warning, the skies were filled with Allied airplanes raining bombs on them, the factory buildings, and the hangars full of parked planes. The bonfire became a target for the Allied warplanes. Three planes buzzed over their heads, and bombs fell all around the potato roast. All of the guards ran, but, amazingly, not a single Jew moved away. Harry and friends went on cooking and eating and dancing. One of the few remaining guards was heard to say, "If you guys have the guts to sit here while the bombs fall, then enjoy your potatoes."

The rumor of an American invasion appeared now to be fact. The prisoners gained hope that the Germans were losing the war.

When the bombing finally stopped, it was near dawn. The ranking officers ordered the soldiers to gather up the three hundred workers in a line and proceed to march them out of camp. Harry was convinced that the Germans would not allow them to reach the next destination, and that this would be a death march.

Harry and Peretz made their way to the front of the line, knowing from previous experience that those in the rear were usually in the most danger. They had marched for perhaps an hour, through a lush valley in farm country, when Harry heard the first shots ring out from the very back of the line. Six or eight more shots followed, and he knew that this was the end. He wondered if they would be shot one by one or in a group. He made up his mind not to wait to find out.

"Peretz," he said, "if we don't do something, we are dead men."

"But what?"

Harry turned to another friend walking with them. "We are dead men if we don't get out of here," he said.

"Can we run?"

"I'm not going to run," said Peretz. "We don't know for sure they will kill us."

"Can't you hear?"

"They've already killed some of us?"

"Me, I'm going to run," said Harry.

"I'm with you," said the friend.

"You, Peretz?" asked Harry.

"No, I only know they will kill you for sure if you run."

"Peretz, we are coming to a wooded area near those trees ahead. We can make a run for it there."

"Not me," said Peretz.

"Tell me when," said the friend.

Several moments later, Harry motioned a ready signal, and he took off toward thick trees. His friend followed. They got a good start, but they had to run uphill.

Then the sound of gunfire rang out.

They didn't stop. They did reach the crest of the hill, but then the ground exploded around them. Harry tripped, and he heard his friend groan as dirt and blood filled the air.

There was a foxhole several feet away. Harry's friend was about to fall down right ahead of him, so he pushed him in the direction of the hole in the ground and jumped in beside him. His friend's blood poured all over Harry. He was not sure whether he was bleeding too. His friend's body felt like dead weight on him, and he buried his face in his wounds.

Within a minute, he heard soldiers approaching. Two soldiers with machine guns came to the edge of the foxhole and looked in. Harry heard one soldier loading his gun, and he lay as still as he could, prepared to die.

"Ah, don't waste any more bullets," Harry heard a second soldier say. "They're already dead."

Harry heard the soldiers leave, but he was afraid to move until he was sure. He took great pains to emerge from the foxhole slowly, peering out from underneath his dead friend's body and then trying to stand.

He felt cold, and he ran his hands along his body to see if he had been shot. He was wet with blood, but unhurt. He felt waves of exhaustion, sadness and loneliness. For the first time in four years, he was free, but it filled him with anger. He thought of his brother still marching with the other prisoners, and then found himself wondering about his mother, sisters, and other family members, and then finally about Leah. He cursed at God and the world for his suffering.

•   •   •

The sun was setting. Harry walked into the darkness of the Bohemian Forest, where he lay down under a tree, covered himself with fallen leaves and branches, and tried to stay warm. He fell asleep with the familiar feeling of hunger.

After several days in the forest, Harry came upon the Regen River, where he thought he might bathe and search for food. As he moved closer, he heard a man's voice singing in German. The man was standing in the river, waist deep, busily washing himself. The sun was not very warm, and Harry knew the man would not be in the water too long.

Harry approached, slowly, cautiously, and without making a

sound. He noticed the man's clothing by a tree near the water's edge. He crept close to the belongings and saw that it was the uniform of an SS man, a handgun in a holster and a rifle propped between the boots.

Harry grabbed the rifle, pointed it at the unsuspecting SS man, and pulled the trigger.

That shot missed, and the naked soldier came running toward him. Harry reached for the handgun and emptied the contents of the chamber into his target. The soldier was probably dead, but Harry was blind with rage. He battered the man's skull with the butt of the rifle until it was a bloody, pulpy stump.

The SS man had rations of food and water near the clothing, and Harry sat under the tree and nourished himself. He removed his bloody clothing and washed himself in the river. He dressed himself in the soldier's uniform, baggy on his 110-pound frame. He pulled an eye patch out of the shirt pocket and placed it on his left eye to complete the disguise. He gathered the soldier's remaining personal belongings and continued on his way.

Hours later, he was deep in farm country. He knew he would soon need food and water, so the farmhouse up ahead was a welcome sight. He walked through the fields and toward the house, passing the horses that were lazily grazing nearby.

He approached the small house with a triangular wooden frame. He went up to the door, knocked, and braced to present himself as a German soldier.

He knocked again, and after several anxious minutes, an elderly man answered the door in his overalls and horn-rimmed glasses.

"What do you want?" the elderly man asked Harry, in a voice full of distrust.

"Can you help me? I am hurt." Harry answered in his best German. He pointed to the eye patch.

The old man looked at Harry suspiciously. "What can I do?"

"I am hurt and tired and I need some food and a place to rest."

An elderly woman came to the door.

"Who are you?" she asked.

"Please help me. We were attacked by Russians and I became separated from my regiment," Harry begged. "I am hungry."

The old couple started to argue with each other, but then they opened the door wide.

"Come in, soldier, of course we will help you," said the man.

The couple took Harry to a bedroom and showed him the bath. The woman opened a drawer in the dresser and gave Harry two fresh towels and some soap.

Harry bathed and dressed again in the uniform.

The old woman knocked on the bedroom door, and walked in carrying a tray full of food. On it were some things Harry had not seen in years scrambled eggs, coffee, bread and butter, jam, and some pieces of pork.

The husband entered the room. Harry sat down and began to eat. The couple watched him, so he refrained from grabbing all the food at once, and he tried to appear refined. He was uncomfortable, and did not speak to the couple as he ate the delicious food.

Harry was afraid to close his eyes and fall asleep, but he was overcome by the comfort of a bed and a full stomach. He stayed alone in the room all evening and through the night and awoke in the morning from a dream that found him in the camp barracks. He was filled with fear and sure that the old couple had seen through his disguise. He had not been careful enough, he feared, and they may have seen the tattooed numbers on his forearm.

He worried that they may have called for help while he was asleep.

Then he heard a knock on his door. It was the old man checking on him.

"Would you like to come to the kitchen for breakfast?" he asked.

"Yes. I will need a few minutes to dress."

Harry put his uniform back on, complete with holster and eye patch, and then went into the kitchen. The old man was sitting at the table being served by his wife. Harry sat down.

"Tell me," said the old man sounding curious, "What regiment are you with?"

Harry lied, "South," he said.

"And what happened to your eye?"

"Shrapnel from an explosion."

Harry was reaching. It was not easy to answer complicated questions; his German was not that good, and the more he spoke, the less fluent he knew he sounded.

"You were not wearing the patch when I came into the room. I saw no wound."

The old woman poured Harry a cup of coffee, and left the room. The questions got tougher to answer. He knew the uniform did not fit, and his German accent was not convincing. He wondered where the old woman had gone.

The old man kept badgering Harry with questions until Harry lost his mind. He pulled out the revolver and shot the old man in the face; his head exploded and blood splattered everywhere.

The old woman ran into the kitchen to see what the commotion was, and Harry shot her too. She hit the floor and was still moving, so Harry fired another shot into her.

Harry ran back to his room, pulled the sheet off the bed, and grabbed the rifle and the rest of the soldier's belongings. He ran back to the kitchen, filled the sheet with food from the cupboards, and exited quickly.

Harry hid in the forest for weeks until he ran out of food. He knew he would have to find another farm. This time a middle-aged woman answered the door. Harry tried the same routine, telling her that he was injured and separated from his unit while fighting the Russians.

The woman was not fooled by his uniform or by his German.

"You're not a soldier," she said to Harry. "You're not even German."

Harry knew she would turn him in and his mind snapped into a blind rage. He took out his revolver and shot her at point-blank range. He walked past her body and into the house, gun cocked. He found the kitchen and started to fill an empty potato sack with food when he heard a noise.

Harry searched the house and found a boy about twelve years old hiding in a bedroom closet.

"You stay in here," Harry told him, and he shut the boy in the closet. Then he ran.

The Whorehouse

HARRY CONTINUED HIDING in the Bohemian Forest. His escape had taken him east to the outskirts of a city called Regensburg, and he found an abandoned, half-standing farmhouse to hide in. He had no idea that the war had ended; his struggle to survive continued.

One morning he looked out the broken window and saw a small band of men in uniform approaching the building. He grabbed the rifle, loaded it, and then put the revolver in its hiding place, inside a piece of crude wire strapped to his thigh. He was prepared to shoot it out rather than be taken. Then he saw an American flag.

He covered the rifle and left it inside the house. Then he walked outside with his hands raised above his head. The Americans approached him cautiously in case he might be a decoy, shielding more soldiers inside. When they realized he was unarmed, they took note of his ill-fitting uniform and look of fear and motioned him to come forward. Harry dropped to the ground and drew a Star of David in the dirt with his finger, all the while keeping his other arm above his head. He stood up and pointed to the shirt sleeve covering his forearm. He unbuttoned the shirt, slipped it off, and showed the soldiers the numbers tattooed on his skin.

One soldier started asking Harry questions in Yiddish. Harry did not know what to make of this GI who identified himself as a Jew from Chicago named Jeffrey Greenberg, but he felt it would be safe to tell him of his escape from the last camp some fifty miles away. While the other soldiers searched the house, Harry sat on the ground with Greenberg talking and sharing his rations and canteen.

The soldiers instructed Harry to follow them to their jeep, and they drove him to headquarters in Regensburg. Harry was given a shirt, underwear, pants, socks, and shoes, all army-issue. Greenberg stayed by Harry's side and gave him half a pack of cigarettes, which Harry gratefully accepted. Harry thanked his new friend and tucked the present into his shirt pocket without the least temptation to smoke. Greenberg lit one up and blew the smoke in Harry's direction.

Harry appeared shy to undress, and Jeffrey showed him the way to a small room where he could remove the German uniform from his back and put on fresh clothes. The GI didn't know that Harry's shyness was only to give him time to position the pistol, still on his thigh, beneath his army trousers. He transferred it successfully and no one knew. Harry was invited to join the soldiers for supper, and he blended in with the other soldiers sitting with him for the hour jeep ride to the next town, Straubing.

Straubing's police headquarters had been appropriated by the American soldiers and made into their command post. After supper, Greenberg said good-bye, and Harry found himself with a new group of GIs. He was offered a cigarette, and this time he put it behind his ear and explained he would smoke it later. He turned his attention to a set of pictures of local houses that the soldiers were placing before him on the table. They asked him to pick a house where he would like to live. At random, he pointed to a snapshot of a two-story house.

The soldier who had asked him to choose collected the other photos and said, "Okay, Let's go."

"Where?" Harry asked.

"We'll move you in tonight."

Three soldiers escorted Harry to a jeep, but before they left the headquarters, they all grabbed their rifles. Harry was driven to the address on the back of the photo.

"Wait in the car," said one soldier to Harry. Two of the soldiers positioned themselves at the foot of the walkway, while the other man knocked on the front door.

Harry watched from the vehicle as a well-dressed woman answered the door. The soldier talked with her for several minutes, and then waved to the others to follow him into the house. Before they disappeared inside, one soldier gave Harry a hand signal to continue to wait. Ten minutes passed until the front door opened again.

The woman emerged from the home, struggling to carry two large suitcases. Following closely behind her were four nicely dressed children carrying their own bags and boxes. The soldiers came out carrying only their rifles. They made no attempt to help the woman or her children. Harry watched her walk down the street struggling with her children and their personal belongings in tow.

One soldier signaled for Harry to get out of the car and approach the house. In his best German, mixed with English and using hand signals, he told Harry that the woman was the wife of a ranking SS officer, now captured, and that the house was now

U.S. Army property. The woman was given enough time to leave with whatever she could carry.

"It's your house for now," Harry thought he heard the soldier say. He didn't feel pity for the German woman and her children, and he didn't wonder or care where they would sleep. Instead he wondered if the home he entered had been stolen from a Jewish family, now dead.

The house was large with four bedrooms, a living room, a big kitchen with separate dining area and a library. Harry was given the keys to this castle by the ranking American soldier. He was told to sit down on the living room couch and the soldier proceeded to explain the circumstances.

Sgt. Dickey was the first to speak, using some German and English, with hand gestures. "Everything in this house belongs to us."

"But we need some help from you," said Private Turney.

The third soldier shook his head in agreement, and sat down too.

"How is it I can help you?" asked Harry.

"Well, you know that we're in Germany," said Sergeant Dickey. "The army has rules that prohibit us from fraternizing with the enemy."

Harry looked puzzled. His German-language skills were not the best, and the same could be said for the Americans. He stared at the three faces without a clue as to what they were saying.

Finally, Private Rankin said: "Girls, Harry, girls."

Private Turney made some vulgar gestures and puckered his lips to simulate licking.

"Oh!" Harry said. "You want me to help you meet German girls."

"Right," said Sergeant Dickey, "We have to behave properly in public. Besides, we can't speak the language. But we have cash. We have cigarettes. We have beer."

Harry and the house made a perfect solution for postwar male boredom. Harry was young and handsome and spoke enough German. He could connect the young soldiers with German women whose men were not coming home and to girls who were interested in earning dollars.

It didn't take long for the dream to become reality. The house was soon a home to four or five girls who moved in. The soldiers had access to the women twenty-four hours a day. There was a party every night, and Harry was the designated host, providing liquor, food, and girls, all paid for by the GIs in Straubing. For his trouble, Harry was given a percentage of the money earned by the girls who lived and worked in the house, and he accepted gratuities from the grateful American soldiers.

Within a few weeks, Harry became a celebrity in Straubing. Many soldiers requested their picture taken with Harry and a half-dressed girl, and the photos became a popular souvenir to take home. The house became so well known that soldiers came from outposts hundreds of miles away to spend a wild evening.

One of Harry's guests took his souvenir photo back to his post in the town of Erlangen, about one hundred and twenty miles away, just north of Nuremberg. The soldier shared his picture from the celebrated whorehouse in Straubing with other soldiers, and in turn it was passed around to a group of concentration camp survivors. Incredibly, one Jew who had been liberated by American soldiers after surviving the last death march recognized the smiling face of his brother.

Peretz Haft was overjoyed to find that his brother was alive.

He immediately got directions from the soldier in the photo, and traveled to Straubing. Peretz arrived at the door of the whorehouse one night, and the reunion with his little brother was a jubilant one. Harry gave Peretz a room and a job working in the house. For any man just out of a concentration camp, running a whorehouse was a dream come true. Peretz liked to joke with Harry that the job was more enjoyable than repairing shoes, especially the part where he could "interview" new girls before they started work. Harry was very happy to make Peretz manager of the whorehouse because he had other plans. Harry was able to plan to return to Belchatow to find Leah and search for the rest of their family.

When the day came, Harry filled an empty suitcase with leather scraps and remnant pieces that he had bought and traded for. The leather, to be used for shoes, would bring a good price in Poland. Another suitcase was used for his personal belongings, and some food for the trip.

There was a daily, free train returning refugees to Poland from Regensburg. A friend drove Harry from Straubing to Regensburg in the sidecar of his motorcycle. The free train in Regensburg turned out to be another boxcar ride, only this time with ten to twenty people boarded comfortably in each car.

The train ride took three or four days to reach Lodz. It stopped many times to pick up and drop off passengers. When Harry arrived in Lodz, he took a taxi to a soap factory that was owned before the war by his cousins Hanna and Aaron. The factory was still standing, although no longer in business, and Harry found Hanna and Aaron at the address he had visited as a child. He was welcomed by his cousins and he stayed overnight with them. From them, he heard the grim news about his family. His brothers Aria and Machel vanished and never returned. Rumor had it that they joined the underground resistance and were killed in a skirmish. His relatives also knew that Birach was dead. After conscription in the Russian army, he had risen in the ranks to become a colonel, but was killed in the battle for Berlin. Sisters Brandel and Rifka and Harry's mother were with the last of the Jews taken from Belchatow. They were gassed in Treblinka.

In the morning, Harry went into town and sold his leather. He returned to Hanna and Aaron, and gave them some of the money. Then he boarded a bus for Belchatow. His relatives knew nothing of Leah's fate or that of her family. He would go and see for himself if she was alive or dead.

When Harry arrived in Belchatow, he went to the home of Leah's Polish girlfriend, Zosha Kubiak. Because the Kubiaks were Christian, their home was still there, and Harry went directly there. Harry knocked on the door, and Zosha answered. He introduced himself and was welcomed into their home. Harry thanked Zosha for delivering his letters from Poznan, and he questioned her about the whereabouts of Leah and her family.

Zosha gave Harry both good and bad news. Leah and her family had escaped with the help of the Polish underground. She knew for sure that Leah had not been taken by the Nazis, but she could not tell Harry where they went, or whether they were still alive. For Harry, after such a long time, the news was more good than bad, and he felt optimistic that with some effort, he might find her. After all, Peretz had found him from a photo, and it gave him reason to hope.

After the visit with Zosha, Harry wandered around the streets of Belchatow. The house he had grown up in was occupied by a poor Polish Christian family. Harry was surprised that very few Jews returned to Belchatow. It was as though the town had been purged of any last remnants of the way things had been.

Harry walked through the downtown market area where he had hustled for pennies as a child. He thought he recognized a familiar face in the crowded market stalls, and he followed the man for several blocks. It was Mischa, the Jewish cop from the coal mines of Jaworzno, who had tormented him on the chain gang. Mischa took a turn down a deserted street, and Harry ran up behind him and tapped him on the shoulder. "I thought it was you," he said, and tried to control his feeling of rage.

"Hertzka, it's so good to see you well."

Before he could finish the sentence, Harry grabbed him and threw him into two garbage cans lined against a wall in the alley. He stood over him and said, "You mean you are surprised to see me alive?" He picked up a garbage can and started to beat him with it. "Do you want to kick me now?" he yelled.

"Please, Hertzka. We all did what we had to do to survive," said Mischa.

Harry started beating him again with the lid of the can until Mischa begged him to stop. He stopped. Mischa lay there bleeding. He let out a sigh of relief that Harry had stopped the beating.

Harry pulled out his revolver and said, "Mischa, now it is your time to die."

Harry enjoyed watching Mischa beg and plead for his life, but he pulled the trigger anyway.

The gun did not fire. Harry cursed and pulled the trigger again.

Again, it only clicked.

"Maybe it is not your time to die. Next time, you may not be so lucky." He pulled him up, all the while pointing the pistol.

Mischa ran down the street. Harry pointed the gun at a trash-can and pulled the trigger. This time it fired.

Harry never ran into Mischa again.

Heavyweight Champion

HARRY CAME BACK to Straubing and shared the bad news about the family with Peretz. He also returned to find that the whorehouse was out of business. The U.S. Army had put a stop to having girls in the house, and in its place had set up a repatriation center for displaced persons to register for transportation home.

With his only source of income gone, Harry needed to find work. Sergeant Dickey was there to provide it. He had contacts in the PX in Straubing who provided boxes of American cigarettes, each box containing twelve cartons with twenty individual packs of American brands inside. Dickey turned the inventory over to Harry, who sold them in the DP [displaced persons] camps for fifty cents a pack, and they split the take three ways.

The smuggling was penny ante at first, but cigarettes were a hot commodity, and soon the thievery became a big business. PX insiders planned to steal a truckload of cigarettes from an upcoming train shipment of goods due in Straubing. Harry would be sent to Berlin, where packs of cigarettes were selling for two dollars each.

The soldiers trusted Harry to drive their haul to Berlin, sell it all, and come back with the cash. Harry was given an army-issued vehicle containing the stolen goods, and within days he had sold out his inventory in the displaced camps in Berlin. He returned to

Straubing with a suitcase containing more than a million German marks.

It was dark when he got to his final destination. He was to meet his partners at his house. He pulled up, stopped the truck, and jumped out carrying the suitcase. But before he took his first step into the house, he felt a trap.

Unknown to Harry, Peretz and several cousins who remained in the house were already being detained by the military and German police who busted the smuggling operation. All that was left was to confiscate the loot and arrest the bagman. Harry didn't give them the chance. He dropped the bag on the front porch and ran as fast as he could. He heard someone yelling, "Hold it," and several shots were fired in his direction, but he got away.

When Peretz was taken to court to be tried in the case, the suitcase was presented as evidence against him, but it only contained three thousand German marks. Someone in charge had taken the bulk of the money. Consequently, Peretz was convicted of a lesser offense and had to spend a few weeks in jail.

Harry knew he could not return to Straubing. He knew he would be killed by those who kept the money. He was now a wanted criminal, but he knew the police didn't really want to find him, so he traveled to the Austria-Czech border to Deggendorf. Later he heard from Peretz that Sergeant Dickey was found dead in his cell while awaiting court martial. It was determined to be a suicide, but Harry was sure Dickey had been killed.

In Deggendorf, Harry tried to start a new life and it was here that he felt he might finally rejoin the human race.

It was in the displaced persons camp in Deggendorf that Harry came to the realization that he needed to start his new life in a new place. Harry felt a profound kinship with the American soldiers he met after being liberated from the concentration camp. For many refugees, the first acts of kindness they experienced after years of Nazi brutality came from the GIs. For this reason, and for the fact that many camp survivors were now without family or homes to return to, it was easy to understand that there was a great desire on the part of many Polish refugees to leave Europe. There was an estimated wait of three to four years to gain eligibility status to go to America. However, if the Jewish refugees chose Palestine as their chosen destination, they were able to leave the DP camp and emigrate much faster.

For Austrian refugees, the situation was very different. Most Austrians wanted to return to Austria, so the waiting list for processing applications was less complicated and took about four to six months. In Deggendorf, Harry met an Austrian Jew named Moses Friedler who had completed his application for transit to Palestine but did not have enough money for the trip. Moses offered Harry his identification papers for five hundred dollars. Because Harry believed he was a wanted criminal, he feared using his real name on an application. This appeared to be the only way he might be able to leave the country. Knowing that part of the application was having a sponsor in America, Harry wrote to an uncle living in Paterson, New Jersey, named Samuel Haft.

Harry's uncle wrote that there was a place for him with his family in America, and that they would be on the look out for a Moses Friedler of Austria at the American immigration center.

Now all that was left for Harry was to wait. By a stroke of co-incidence, a friend told him about a Jewish Boxing Championship being organized by American servicemen. It was being well publicized throughout Germany, and the event would be held in Munich, in January 1946.

Föhrenwald, d. 14.3.46

Dear uncle!

I have got your letter and be glad, that Mr. Spiegler
of Brooklin has visit you. He has truely told to you what I am doing here.
In the time when Mr. Spiegler was here I worked-by- in the american company.
Now I am in the jewisch camp in Föhrenwald, thet I can go quicklier to
America.
Dear uncle I have got an letter from Podlowski and thanks him very much
for kixx that which he has done for me. I am glad that he has got my letter
with picture.
I am happy that ixkmmx you knows hhow many people from our family are
on life. I can tell you that our family now is greater because cousin
Hanna has married and the son of your sister has merried too. My brother
wantes to marry in one month. They all wants to marry because they have
no perents.now, and every wishes to get an new family. They all thinks to
drive to Palestina, becaus they have nothing to do here in Germany.
I hope that it would be no long time to get to, you to America.
You askes me in your letter if I need anything to put on or to eat. But I
need nothing because we dont want to have so much things here in Germany
therefore we have not to take all this things with us to America. The same
is with the others. We dont need any mony because we have much.
Every day in Germany is very long and so I beg you to do for me what you
can that I can go to you as quickly as it would go. You knows what we have
had in the concentrations camp, and you will understeand me that I want to
come to you and away from ermany. Every day is so long and we always
remember us on the bad time in the concentrations camp.
Now I want to write you all the formation about myself.
Name: Hertzko Haft
Birth: 28.7.1925
Town of birth: Belchatow Kreis Peatrkow
Fathers full name. Moses Haft
Mothers maiden name: Hinde Waimann
    "   town of birth: Kaminsk Kreis Radomsk 1986
Died in conzentration cam in Tremblinka.

If it is possible to send any wash to put on. My great is 1,78m
By us there gaves nothing news. I wait, all the days of an letter of you
and your family.
Now I want to shut the letter and hope to hear soon from you.
Many wishes on the aunt and your children and the children of them.
I think that I am able to write better in the next letter.
    Now many wishes from

                the son of   your brother

                    Haft Hercko

        ירׁק אַנﬠ רﬠ ﬩ﬠﬦ יﬦו

Harry's letter to Uncle Samuel Haft from a displaced persons camp in
Germany. Courtesy of the author.

Harry took an apartment in the nearby town of Friesing and had several weeks to train for the fights. He heard that the competition would include bouts in all weight classes, from flyweight to heavyweight. Harry weighed about one hundred and sixty pounds, and he decided to sign up for both the light heavyweight and the heavyweight events.

Training for the tournament was the distraction Harry needed from the endless hours of waiting and wondering about his future. He focused on his fighting skills and looked forward to the competition.

The event was a huge success, attended by thousands of American GIs. Harry won all the elimination bouts in both divisions. In the semifinals he knocked out a light heavyweight fighter, and then two hours later knocked out a heavyweight opponent.

The tournament officials would not allow Harry to fight in both weight classes in the finals. Harry had to choose. He decided to fight in the heavyweight division because he felt that the heavyweight bouts were more popular.

In the championship match, Harry swarmed all over his opponent and knocked him out in less than one minute of the first round.

Harry was a proud young man at the awards ceremony. General Lucius Clay, the Army's youngest brigadier general and later known as the architect of the Berlin Airlift, awarded the medals in the center ring. Harry not only received a cup for winning the heavyweight title, but was voted the outstanding boxer of the tournament. He was given a bronze statue of Apollo, inscribed with a record of this achievement.

When Harry was presented with the statue, he took the oppor-

Heavyweight championship winner Harry Haft (center) holding a trophy statue of Apollo. Courtesy of the author.

tunity to show General Clay the numbers on his arm while thanking him.

"General, you know what bad times I have had in Germany. Can you help me get to America?"

"What about your family?" Clay asked.

"There is no one left. There is nothing for me here."

"Come to my office in Munich tomorrow afternoon. I'll see what I can do," and he shook his hand and patted him on the back.

Harry went to the general's office the next afternoon, but he was not in. His assistant made it plain that there was little that Clay could do for him, and that he should register like everyone else. Just four months later, Harry, under an assumed identity, gained passage on the *Marine Marlin,* a troopship operated by the War Shipping Administration of the United States Army to transport refugees, and voyaged from Bremerhaven, Germany, to New York City.

PART TWO
DREAMS

Uncle Sam

HARRY ARRIVED IN AMERICA with one stuffed suitcase filled with his belongings, very little money, and the clothes on his back. The transatlantic trip had taken a week and it had been less than a pleasant voyage. The *Marine Marlin* carried about three hundred refugees. Very few had sleeping quarters, and Harry was one of the many who had to sleep on any available deck space. Except for the few privileged on board who had enough money to eat in the dining room, most of the passengers brought their own food for the trip.

Harry's most prized possession made the journey with him. The bronze statue of Apollo that General Lucius Clay had awarded to him was cradled in his arms for most of the voyage. Harry believed that the statue had great value. It was rumored that the statue had been looted from a European museum by German soldiers and found by American troops who then awarded it as the grand prize for the tournament championships.

Harry was anxious for the ship to dock. Every day on the trip he felt flush with the promise of freedom and opportunity, but the nights were difficult. Every night during the trip, Harry had terrible visions of his time in the camps. When he did fall asleep, he would wake up terrified by nightmares. For him, the most frightening images were the corpses burning in the ovens of

Marine Marlin, the ship that brought Harry Haft to America. Courtesy of the author.

Auschwitz, and he would wake up overcome with the stench of burning flesh. Twenty-three-year-old Harry was going to America, but unfortunately he was unable to leave behind the memories of his bad experiences.

Uncle Samuel Haft came to meet Harry at the Port of New York, where the *Marine Marlin* docked. After processing, Harry met his Uncle Samuel for the first time. Harry really did not know what to expect from his father's oldest brother. He knew very little about his uncle, except for stories he had heard in his youth, told to him by his older brothers.

According to his vague memory of these stories, Harry knew just a few things about Uncle Samuel. He knew he had left for the United States just before he was born. He remembered that his family never spoke kindly about Samuel because he had brought shame to even their low level of society. Samuel was considered the black sheep of the family for marrying Sadie, a known prostitute in Belchatow, and running away from Poland with her. The stories about his uncle didn't matter; Samuel Haft was the only possible American sponsor for Harry to enable him to leave Europe.

Harry and his Uncle Sam became acquainted with each other on the ride to Paterson, New Jersey, where Samuel had his home and his family and his business. Harry learned that in the United States, Uncle Sam was anything but a black sheep. He was a successful businessman and the head of an extended family.

Sam and Sadie lived in a three-family apartment building and had three sons. Phil, the oldest, was a dentist. Nathan owned a shoe store nearby. The youngest, Harry, worked with Sam in their moving and storage company, called Sam Haft and Son. Not to confuse the two Harrys, the family began calling their newly found relative Herschel.

Sam and Sadie made room for Herschel in their first-floor apartment. Cousin Harry lived in his own apartment in the same building, on the second floor, with his wife Bernice, and their two young children, Bruce and Marilyn.

Though Sam made a place for Herschel in his home, Herschel often wondered why Uncle Sam and Cousin Harry did not offer him a job in their moving business. Herschel was young and strong and felt that they could have given him a job loading and unloading trucks. Several weeks passed, and Herschel soon realized that he would have to find work on his own. He began to feel obligated and broke living under their roof.

One day Uncle Sam brought Herschel to the downtown law office of Hy Zimmel, a distant relative who helped correct Herschel's entry papers. A huge sports fan, Hy was intrigued by Herschel's boxing background, and when he learned that Herschel had won a heavyweight championship in Munich, he recognized an opportunity. He called up some friends at the *Paterson Evening News*, one of North Jersey's largest newspapers, and the next day there was an article in the paper about Herschel with the headline, "Heavyweight Champion arrives from Germany." The article was a short piece describing Harry "Herschel" Haft, a Jewish refugee who fought seventy-five matches to a finish in the Nazi horror camps before winning championships in Munich and coming to this country.

Two days after the article appeared in the newspaper, on an uneventful Sunday afternoon, two gruff-looking men knocked on the door of Uncle Sam's apartment.

When Sam opened the door, one man stepped forward and introduced himself. "Hello, how do you do? I'm Frank Palermo. I've come all the way from Philadelphia to speak to Harry Herschel. Business."

"Business?"

"I'm a fight manager. I'd like to talk to the kid if I can. Is he here?"

Uncle Sam hesitated to let them in. "He's not here," Sam explained, "I don't know when he's coming back."

Actually, Harry was spending the afternoon at a local gym, but Sam didn't like the looks of these strangers, and he said, "He could be gone for a couple of days. I'm his uncle, can I help you?"

"We'd like to talk to him about getting in the fight game here in America. There's money to be made."

"Is there a phone number? I can have him call you when he returns. He should be back by Friday."

"Here, let me write it down for you," said Frank Palermo, and he turned to his cohort to get a pen. He wrote down the number on a piece of scrap paper and handed it back to Uncle Sam.

"Blinky, I'm not driving back to Philly without getting something to eat," said Frank Palermo's cohort.

"Relax, relax. We'll stop at a diner."

Frank Palermo then said to Sam, "Listen, have him call me collect."

The men left.

When Herschel returned, he found his uncle livid.

"Who the hell you hanging around with?" he asked Herschel when he came through the door.

Herschel was taken by surprise. "What do you mean?" he asked.

"You listen to me. I've been in America for twenty years and I've never seen a gangster, and now you've got them knocking on my door?" he said with his eyebrows raised. "Frank Palermo, a fight manager, was here looking for you."

"What did he want?"

"Nothing. I told him you weren't interested."

Herschel immediately realized that the visit was the result of the newspaper article. The next day he took the bus over to Zimmel's office. Herschel had been working out in the gym that morning, and his muscles were rippling through the tight T-shirt he wore. Seeing his powerful physique, Zimmel was impressed. Hy saw real potential in Herschel, and when he learned of the visit from the fight manager, he knew he had to act. He explained to Herschel that as a lawyer and part of the family, he would be the best person to represent him. He instructed Herschel not to talk to anyone in the fight game, and he quickly drew up a contract placing himself in control of the rights to Harry "Hershel" Haft, the fighter. He handed Herschel the hastily drawn agreement and said, "Look Herschel, I know your uncle. He wouldn't have a problem with you fighting if I were in charge. I'm going to get you started. I'm going to find you a manager, support your training and we'll all make some money. Trust me." He put a pen in Herschel's hand. Herschel signed the paper, and they shook hands and hugged.

Zimmel had a hard time getting Herschel caught up in his fantasies of a boxing championship, of fame and notoriety. Sure, Herschel was excited about his prospects, but unlike Zimmel, he imagined that his fame might serve another purpose. Any publicity he could get from boxing, Herschel thought, might give him the opportunity and resources to reunite with Leah, if she were alive. His search for her in postwar Poland and Germany had been fruitless, yet he still had hope. He had not been able to confirm her placement in a camp, or her death.

He wondered: Could she have survived? Could she have somehow found her way to America too? Harry imagined himself as famous as Joe Louis. If he could be a champion, Leah might see his name in a newspaper, or see him on television, and know he was looking for her.

Zimmel would not let Harry take the bus home, and had his secretary drive him to the apartment. Harry thanked the secretary and turned and climbed the short flight of stairs into the hallway outside Uncle Sam's apartment. He found his Aunt Sadie in the kitchen cutting up carrots for a soup.

"Got me a job," said Harry with a sheepish grin.

"Wonderful. What will you be doing?" asked Aunt Sadie.

Harry waved his boxing contract at her.

"And what's that?" she asked.

"My contract. I'm going to prizefight."

"What?" Sadie responded in a tone of disbelief.

"I'm going to box."

Aunt Sadie now wore a horrified expression.

"Herschel, didn't you go through enough punishment?"

"Aunt Sadie," Harry tried to reassure her, "After all I've been through, what harm can a man with gloves on his hands do to me?"

Aunt Sadie continued to shake her head disapprovingly, so Harry went to his room.

Uncle Samuel came home later that evening. When Sadie told him about Harry's plans, he lost his temper. He yelled for Herschel to come to the living room.

"Sit down," Samuel instructed.

Harry sat on the couch.

"You listen to me. You want to be a prizefighter?"

"Yes."

"Then you pack up your stuff and get out. Find another place to live."

"But Uncle . . ."

"Pack your bags now. I don't want any more visits from your gangster friends."

"But, my contract is with your cousin Hy."

"I don't care who it's with. I didn't bring you over here to be a fighter. When I come home from work tomorrow, you need to be gone." Aunt Sadie did not come to Herschel's defense.

Harry telephoned Zimmel and told him what happened. Zimmel came by the next morning to speak with Uncle Sam. He brought with him Harry Mandell, a small-time talent agent, and introduced him. Uncle Samuel had left for work, so Mandell was only able to meet Aunt Sadie.

"Aunt Sadie, meet Harry Mandell, he's going to be Herschel's manager. I'm disappointed Sam isn't here to meet him."

Aunt Sadie seemed somewhat surprised to find that Harry Mandell was a nicely dressed Jewish businessman.

"Does he look like a gangster to you?" Zimmel asked.

"No. Look Hy," Sadie explained, "Samuel wants no part of the fight business. If Herschel's going to be a fighter, it's not going to be under our roof."

She gave her nephew a last hug and wished him luck. Zimmel and Mandell helped Herschel with his belongings. They loaded his gear into the trunk of Mandell's big black 1946 Ford Sedan. Harry was impressed by the vehicle with its giant whitewall tires and moon hubcaps, and he believed Mandell to be rich.

Mandell drove Zimmel back to his office in Paterson. It was agreed on the ride that Herschel's fight name would be Harry "Herschel" Haft. Mandell told Zimmel that he would find an affordable room for Harry somewhere in Brooklyn.

Mandell and Harry drove off in the black Ford to Coney Island where Mandell checked Harry into the Half Moon Hotel. They went up to the front desk, and Mandell inquired of the clerk, "See this tough guy. Can we put him on the sixth floor?"

"I got a room for him," said the desk clerk.

Mandell turned to Harry and said, "You know about the sixth floor don't you?"

"No."

"Well, a few years back, a guy by the name of Abraham 'Kid Twist' Reles was gonna testify against the gangsters—Jews from Brownsville known as Murder, Inc."

"You mean Jewish gangsters?"

"Yeah. But he never got to testify. He was under police protection and one morning he goes out the sixth-floor window . . . splat . . . dead."

"Did the cops kill him?" asked Harry.

"You know anybody who jumps out a window because they want to?"

"No."

Here was Harry's introduction to Brooklyn. He was new in this country and unfamiliar with the ways of organized crime here. Although he had yet to meet a "gangster," he felt relieved to find out that some of the gangsters in this country were Jewish.

Two days later, Mandell moved Harry into a boardinghouse on Seventh Street near Brighton Beach. Mandell took Harry shopping for clothes so that Harry could look more "American." It was June, Harry was twenty-three, and there was no better place to be than on Brighton Beach, where he could stay in shape running along the beach while eyeing all the pretty girls.

Training

ON A WARM DAY in the first week of June 1948, Mandell pulled up in front of Harry's boardinghouse in Brighton Beach. Harry was standing outside, waiting.

"Get in the car," said Mandell.

"Where are we going?" asked Harry.

"We're going up to Greenwood Lake. I want to introduce you to some people in the fight game."

Teddy Gleason's boxing training camp at the Brown's Hotel at Greenwood Lake, near Hewitt, New Jersey, was a mecca for fighters training for important matches. Mandell knew that Harry needed a good trainer, and was told that some of the best trainers were working at the Lake. Mandell and Harry arrived at the facility and walked into the gym in their street clothes. The gym was very crowded, mobbed with fighters working out and their fans.

"Lotta people here. What the hell is going on here?" Mandell asked himself as they walked in the door.

There was a big crowd around a training ring, and it was difficult to get close.

"What's going on?" Mandell asked another guy in street clothes.

"Rocky Graziano's sparring. He's up here training for his fight with Tony Zale next week."

"Thanks. Harry, let's go over there, see if we can squeeze in, and take a look."

Mandell and Harry watched Graziano go a couple of rounds. When Graziano was done, Mandell began working the gym like it was a cocktail party. He brought Harry with him everywhere and introduced him to anyone who looked like a fighter or trainer. Harry was a pretty impressive sight, all tanned and in great shape from running miles along the Coney Island beach.

Mandell recognized Whitey Bimstein, one of the best trainers in the business, walking around the gym. Mandell knew how to talk someone up, and he began working on Whitey. Bimstein stood there scratching his bald head and listening to Mandell's relentless sales pitch.

"Well, if your guy's so good, let's see what he looks like in the ring," Whitey said in a soft but challenging tone.

Bimstein arranged for an assistant to lend Harry sparring gear. Harry changed into the borrowed trunks, T-shirt, cup, and headgear. Bimstein taped Harry's hands and laced up the big twelve-ounce training gloves. Harry was all ready to go, except for the proper footwear. No one had a pair of shoes his size, so he entered the ring in his socks.

Bimstein introduced Harry to Dick Wagner, a veteran light heavyweight, who was dressed and ready to spar. Wagner did not care who Harry was; he was not particular who he sparred with. As a matter of fact, Harry detected a smirk on Wagner's face beneath the headgear, which told him that Wagner intended to make him his next punching bag. Bimstein told both fighters to go easy.

Wagner went right at Harry, trying to land a big punch and knock the new guy out. He started a slugfest. Harry quickly realized that sparring to Dick Wagner was just an opportunity to knock someone out. Fighting toe-to-toe was Harry's European style of boxing. Harry never backed up, and the two fighters exchanged blow after blow. In a matter of minutes, the crowd watching Graziano sensed the action and started watching the two fighters. Even Graziano and his manager Eddie Coco looked on.

Bang.

Harry knocked Dick Wagner down. Wagner got up on one knee, took a breath, and rose, ready to continue the battle. Bimstein saw that the workout had progressed into a war, and he stepped in to stop the sparring before either fighter got hurt. Harry went to the showers to put on his street clothes.

"What do you think?" Mandell asked Bimstein.

"He's flatfooted. He's going to get hit. He's got no style."

"Say something nice."

"He can hit and take a punch, but he's real green and needs plenty of work."

"Okay?"

"Bring him over to Stillman's and we'll see."

"Okay."

"I'll tell Freddy [Brown] about him."

After Bimstein finished talking to Mandell, Eddie Coco came over.

"You got a contract with this guy?" Coco inquired.

"Yep."

"I can get you thirty thousand for him."

"He's not for sale, but I'll talk with my partner."

Mandell and Harry stayed the night at Brown's. After breakfast, they drove back to New York. Mandell stopped off at the Everlast factory in the Bronx. Harry was treated to all the courtesies given to professional boxers. He was given all of his boxing equipment, headgear, shorts, gloves, robes, cups, and shoes for free by Everlast for promotional purposes. The clerk asked about Harry's accent, and when he heard Harry's story, he had a white Star of David stitched on his purple fight trunks. The Jewish emblem on his trunks was very important to Harry, who wanted to be known as a Jewish fighter.

In mid-June, Harry's training began in earnest. Every day he traveled by train from his room near Brighton Beach to Stillman's Gym on 54th and Broadway. Harry was a new face at Stillman's, and Jack Curley, the doorman, tried to get fifty cents from him to enter. Harry did not have any spare change, and Curley just refused to let him in. Twenty minutes later, Mandell arrived and paid Harry's monthly training fee.

Once inside, Mandell sought out Freddy Brown, Bimstein's partner. Freddy was not hard to spot. He had the flattened nose and telltale eyes of an ex-fighter, not to mention the burning cigar in his mouth. There was plenty of cigarette smoke in that gym, as well as the smell of sweat and grit coming from the wall to wall bodies. Harry bummed a cigarette off someone and got acquainted with his new surroundings, while Mandell spoke to Freddy.

"Is this the kid from Germany that Whitey called me about?"

"He's here in the flesh." Mandell called Harry over.

"Harry, this is Freddy Brown."

"Good to meet you." said Harry.

"Whitey sends me all the young guys. He's so busy these days."

"And you're his manager?"

"Harry Mandell," said Harry and he stuck out his hand.

"How much time you want from me?" asked Freddy Brown.

Mandell hesitated. He knew that time meant money, and if he could pay Brown, Brown would have time to help Harry. Mandell knew he did not have much money for training. He was hoping that Harry would impress them enough to get him a few quick fights to pay the bills. He did not know what to say and was silent.

"All right, I know you're just getting started. I'm going to take Harry around, show him where everything is, and give him a routine."

After a couple of days of Harry working out on his own, Brown called him over.

"Harry, let's see what you can do in the ring. Get your gear on. You're going to spar with Green."

Harry and Harold Green had time to talk before stepping into the ring. Green spoke to Harry in Yiddish. Harold asked about the numbers on his arm, about his time in the concentration camps. He was curious about what it was like, and how he had survived. They became instant friends. Harold told him about what it took to survive in the fight game in New York. After all, Green, from Brooklyn, was a world-ranked middleweight contender. He confided that he was paid to lose to Rocky Graziano in 1945, after beating him twice before. He told Harry that his biggest regret was letting his friends down. The way Harold put it to Harry, he "buried half of Brownsville," friends who bet on him to win, when he went down.

Green went easy on the inexperienced Harry in the sparring ring. Freddy saw for himself that Harry was a very raw boxer. After each sparring session, he would patiently explain to Harry what he was doing wrong. Freddy seemed to repeat the same advice over and over, and he began to wonder why Harry kept making the same mistakes. Brown started to think Harry might not be worth his time.

In mid-July, Bimstein took a second look at Harry. Bimstein matched Harry up with Artie Levine, a prominent light heavyweight, or perhaps big middleweight.

Levine and Harry went at it as though it were a real fight. The handful of spectators sitting on benches and folding chairs really got into the slugging. Levine was fast. He was too fast for Harry. In the third round, Harry knocked Levine through the ropes. Levine came back angry and started rocking Harry. Levine was the hardest puncher to ever hit Harry in the gym. Again, Bimstein called the slugfest to a halt.

"I told you guys to go easy. Don't get yourselves hurt," screamed Bimstein.

Whitey grabbed Harry's arm and pulled him aside. Ordinarily, Whitey was a patient man, but this time he chewed Harry out for not protecting himself properly.

"If you're gonna let someone hit you five times to get one punch in, you're gonna get killed."

By the end of the month, Mandell was able to get Harry a real fight. It was time for him to stop sparring, and start earning, as money was in short supply.

Harry's first fight was against Jimmy Letty on August 6, 1948, in Staten Island. Harry flattened Letty in the second round. Some thought it was an impressive debut because Letty had gone the distance three times with highly regarded Bernie Reynolds. After the fight, Mandell handed Harry seventy dollars, his share of the purse.

A week later, on August 13, Harry fought Gilbert Cardione in

Lodi, New Jersey. After a feel-out first round, Harry pummeled Cardione and knocked him out in round two. After the fight, Mandell gave Harry sixty dollars as his take.

Twelve days after the Cardione fight, on August 25, 1948, Mandell drove Harry upstate to Utica, New York, for a fight with Billy West. Harry battled West for six rounds and earned a unanimous decision. On the ride back following the fight, Mandell handed Harry forty dollars and said, "Here is yours, less your share of travel expenses."

Harry nearly exploded. Driving morning till late night, going six rounds, getting beat up for the third week in a row made him boil. "Three fights in a month and I'm still broke," said Harry, trying to calm down.

"We got three wins. We're gonna get better fights now, you'll see," promised Mandell.

"I can't even find my name in the papers, before or after a fight," Harry grumbled. If only he had gotten some publicity, he could've swallowed the poor pay.

After the West fight, Harry took some extra time off to enjoy the Labor Day weekend crowds at Brighton Beach. The weather along the ocean was surprisingly nice considering a hurricane was brewing further down the coast in New Orleans. Harry took long walks to Nathan's at Coney Island and ate hotdogs and frozen custard.

Harry went back to his daily train ride to Stillman's, meeting Mandell at the gym most every day. The training was not going any better than before his three wins. Word was that Harry had beaten three losers, and now he was bigheaded and even less receptive to learning than before.

Bimstein and Brown were not making much money from

Harry's fights, and Mandell was not throwing them any extra money in the gym, so Harry did not get much of their attention. Plus, Harry had a bad temper and nobody wanted to spar with him because he would try to knock his opponent's head off.

There were only two boxers in Stillman's gym who were willing to spar with Harry. Both of these men went on to fight for the heavyweight championship of the world.

Lee Oma was a heavyweight who could take all of Harry's best shots, and return even bigger ones. When Oma bragged to Harry that he and Jake LaMotta were partners in a whorehouse in Miami, Harry told Oma about his house in Germany and they exchanged funny stories about the working women they knew.

Roland LaStarza was another world-class fighter who did not fear sparring with Harry. Harry and Roland became good friends. Harry admired Roland because he was a college student at the City College of New York, and in the ring, Roland would turn out to be the smartest boxer Harry ever worked with.

LaStarza told Harry to go easy or pull punches. Harry was not embarrassed that he found LaStarza too fast for him to hit because LaStarza was too fast for anybody to hit. Harry could have learned how to protect himself in the ring from LaStarza, but he was not a good pupil.

As the days and weeks went on, Bimstein and Brown paid very little attention to Harry. Mandell would argue with both trainers about their neglect of his fighter, but Harry did not know that he was being neglected because the trainers were not being paid. When Mandell stopped paying the six dollar monthly gym fee, Harry was kicked out of Stillmans.

Harry stayed in Brighton Beach and started feeling sorry for himself. He was so broke that he had to borrow money for food from Cousin Phil, the dentist. He was sure word got back to Uncle Samuel about his troubles, but he never heard from him.

Mandell called Harry on the telephone at the boarding house and told him about a gym on 125th Street in Harlem.

"You ever been to Harlem?" asked Mandell.

"No."

"There's this gym in Harlem. Fella by the name of Bill Miller is the trainer over there. Ever hear of Sugar Ray Robinson?"

"Sure, who hasn't?"

"Well, he taught him how to fight."

Harry was only mildly inspired. Mandell continued, "Think of what he could do for us, huh? Let me tell you how to get there by train," and Mandell gave Harry instructions.

"How do I pay to get in?" asked Harry.

"The people up in Harlem will let you train practically for free. All the schvartzes are up there, Harry. They're as broke as you are."

Harlem

IT'S A LONG WAY from Brighton Beach to Harlem, Harry thought to himself while riding the subway, crossing New York City boroughs and cultures. Harlem's main thoroughfare, 125th Street, was bustling with people and activity. The gym was just a few blocks from the subway train, and Harry found it easily.

He walked into the gym clutching his Everlast equipment bag. For a moment time stopped as he looked around. The gym was large, with two main rings, but it was not nearly as crowded as Stillman's. He noticed that some of the boxers, who had been hitting punching bags, stopped to stare at him. He realized that he was getting long looks from the other fighters because he was the only white man in the gym.

"Looking for Bill Miller," Harry said to a man leaning against the wall smoking a cigarette.

"Over there," he pointed to an older man untangling knots in a bunch of worn gloves.

Harry went over.

"Are you Bill Miller?"

"Miller's on vacation. What do you need him for?"

"My manager told me to see Bill Miller."

"You from Harry Mandell?"

"Yes."

"Ok, so I am Bill Miller. No one told me you were white. I was expecting a Negro fighter. What's your name, kid?"

"Harry Haft."

"Where you from with that accent?"

"Poland and Germany," said Harry.

"You fight before?"

"In Germany and here. I got three wins."

"Don't be shy around me," Miller playfully slapped Harry on the shoulder. "You can call me Pops."

Harry sensed that Miller took a liking to him. Minutes later, Mandell arrived. He handled all of the business with Miller. That meant he paid Harry's training fees, which were quite a bit less than at Stillman's. He also worked out a percentage deal with Miller for him to be in Harry's corner during matches. Mandell knew that Miller would give Harry the attention he was not getting at Stillman's.

Miller made Harry feel right at home in the gym. Harry had been in the United States for only a short time and didn't fully understand the racial issues that made him a target in the gym. Some fighters would tell Harry to go back downtown, but Harry was a tough guy who could not be intimidated, and he just ignored them. This treatment was nothing compared to the hatred and the antagonism he experienced in Europe.

Nonetheless, Bill Miller did not want any trouble among his fighters, so he decided to introduce Harry to Coley Wallace, a black fighter he knew wouldn't resent Harry's presence in the gym.

Coley was a recent Golden Gloves heavyweight champion. He was a six-foot-two, two-hundred pound true heavyweight, who was training every day but not actively fighting. He looked so

Fighters Randy Turpin, Coley Wallace, and Joe Louis.
Courtesy of *The Ring*.

much like Joe Louis, the heavyweight champ, that he portrayed him in the 1953 film *The Joe Louis Story*.

Coley and Harry struck up an instant friendship. Bill Miller matched Coley up as Harry's sparring partner. Every trainer wants to see a fighter in the ring, and Miller was no exception.

"Harry, get your stuff on. You'll go two rounds with Coley," he said on Harry's first day in the gym.

Harry got dressed. Unlike Stillman's, there was no line for the sparring ring. Despite free admission to observe sparring, there was never a big crowd.

Miller stood on the ring apron, while Coley and Harry climbed into the ring. Coley motioned for Harry to come close.

When he was in earshot, Coley leaned over and said in a soft voice, "Look here white boy. We're not getting paid, so we don't hit hard. Got it?"

Harry looked over at Miller who hung on the ropes and smiled.

"We're not going to hit hard," Harry repeated to Miller.

For a big man, Coley moved fast and used the whole ring. Harry began chasing him but was not effective. Coley moved in closer. Coley clearly had more refined boxing skills and peppered Harry with jab after jab. Harry practiced defense and Coley began throwing combinations. Coley scored with some pretty hard punches to the head. After getting hit a few times, Harry forgot himself and started to fight back. He threw several hard punches that landed and Coley stepped back and stopped fighting.

"Hold it," Coley yelled.

Harry looked puzzled.

"Hold it," repeated Coley.

Harry stopped and put his arms down.

"What I tell you? You understand my English? I said we ain't getting paid for this. So we don't hit hard," Coley said.

Harry apologized.

They picked up the sparring. Coley delivered a crushing combination of blows, then danced away before Harry could hit back. Miller saw that Harry was getting mad, so he stepped into the ring and ended the session.

Miller unlaced Harry's gloves and asked, "What did you learn, son?"

Harry answered, "When he says we don't hit hard, it just means me."

Bill Miller could not stop laughing, but he went on to give Harry a long lecture on all the things he was doing wrong in the ring.

Coley worked out with Harry every day. Coley had a big heart and knew that Harry was dead broke. The Wallace family's home was just a few blocks from the gym, and Coley took Harry there every day for lunch. On some days, Harry's best meal would be at Coley's place, and when Harry was short on subway fare to get back and forth to Brighton Beach, Coley would find a couch for Harry to sleep on.

The Wallace family was seemingly well-to-do. They lived in a large apartment with nice furnishings. They also had a maid and a cook. When Harry slept over, he would have his dinner with the family. Coley's father loved to talk about boxing. Mr. Wallace was a big Joe Louis fan, and he would reminisce about every round and every fight Louis fought.

Coley's father wanted Harry to explain why white people didn't want Joe Louis as the Champ. Harry had no answers. He was too new in the country to be able to answer that question.

Miller, who would get a piece of Harry's purse, helped arrange a fight at the Jamaica Arena in Queens for Wednesday night, September 22, 1948. Harry could not contain his excitement about the bout. The fight was going to be televised, and finally Harry would be in the public eye. The match pitted Harry, at 174 pounds, against Matt Mincey, who weighed 205 pounds.

Mandell picked up Harry in Brighton Beach and drove out to Queens. Along the way they stopped at a diner for a light meal, where Harry ate a couple of burgers without the bread.

Miller was waiting for Harry to arrive to loosen him up and

put him through a series of light exercises. Miller's assistant gave Harry a liniment rubdown, and then Bill talked Harry through the fight strategy.

When Harry entered the ring, he removed his robe, and walked around in circles, proudly showing off the Star of David on his trunks. The referee motioned both fighters to the center of the ring. Mincey towered over Harry during the pre-fight instructions. For a moment, he reminded Harry of his last fight in the camps against the much larger Frenchman.

When the bell sounded, the two fighters went right at each other. To Harry's surprise, Mincey was just a big, lumbering, slow-moving target, and very vulnerable. In the first minute of the bout, Harry landed several hard blows to Mincey's midsection and then nailed him right on the chin. Mincey went down. Harry prayed that Mincey would get up. The fight was only sixty seconds old, and he didn't want his first appearance on television to end so quickly. Harry was relieved that Mincey did manage to get up.

The fight was a six-rounder, and Harry was determined to get all the exposure he could. He had learned in the camps how to control the length of the fight by playing with an opponent to diminish his skills and then end the fight. This approach drew the anger of his trainer between rounds. At the end of round five, Miller could no longer stand it, and tore into him.

"You son of a bitch!" Miller yelled at Harry, as he wiped the fighter's face with a towel.

Miller gave Harry a slap in the face.

"This ain't a fucking playground!!" Miller continued, with spit spewing with his words.

He forced Harry to look in his eyes.

"You ain't gonna hit him and hold him. What are you gonna

wait for, till he cuts you? I want his black ass on the floor now!" When the bell rang to start round six, Harry quickly knocked Mincey out.

At that moment, Harry Haft became a known fighter. The newspaper and television publicity worked. Harry started getting calls from Jewish refugees who recognized his name. He got a call from a refugee from Belchatow who knew of his family in Poland. Harry asked the caller if he knew any news of Leah and her family. Harry was told that he had little information about her whereabouts, but he believed that she was not taken to Treblinka or Chelmno when the town was evacuated. Harry was convinced that his celebrity would enable him to find her.

Washington, D.C.

MANDELL TOLD HARRY to take a few days off after the Mincey fight. He wanted to get Harry back into Stillman's, where he knew better fight promoters made their matches, but it would take a little politicking on his part. Training in Harlem would get Harry nowhere, he thought, so he called Freddy Brown on the phone and began talking up Harry. His efforts fell short as Freddy was rude and abrupt:

"Who'd Harry beat?" he asked.

"Matt Mincey."

"Matt Mincey's been knocked out by everybody—including his grandmother."

It was not exactly the welcome mat, but by the time Mandell finished the phone conversation Brown was agreeable to having Harry back at Stillman's. This time Mandell promised some money to Brown for his time working with Harry, and Brown assented.

Meanwhile, Harry was enjoying his time off, spreading the hundred-dollar purse as far as he could. Though he was still getting the cold shoulder from Uncle Sam and Aunt Sadie, his cousin Phil, the dentist, invited him to his home in Paterson for dinner. Phil played a supporting role in Harry's boxing career by providing him with custom mouthpieces to protect him in the ring.

On Wednesday, September 29, Mandell called Harry and

asked him if he wanted to take a ride down to Washington, D.C., to attend the Thursday night fights.

Harry was not doing anything else, so he said yes.

"Who's fighting?" Harry asked.

"You know Maxie Shapiro?"

"Sure." All the Jewish boxers knew Maxie. He had fought one hundred and twenty-four fights. This match would be his next to last bout. Maxie had a long career, a good career, but unfortunately, he was best known for being knocked down five times by Sugar Ray Robinson.

"Who's he fighting?"

"Sonny Boy West."

"I never heard of him."

"Young kid. Twenty-three wins. Good fighter. Jack Bluman, Maxie's manager asked me to come."

"Yeah, I'll come. I got nothing better to do."

"It's about a four-hour drive, so I'll pick you up early, about nine."

The next morning Mandell was there promptly at nine o'clock.

"By the way," says Mandell, "we're stopping in the Bronx."

"What for?"

"We're picking up Cardione. The Spanish kid you fought last month."

"What for?"

"He's on the card. He has no manager."

"Are you his manager?"

"Yeah, it'll pay for the gas."

So Mandell picked up Cardione and the three of them drove down to Washington. Harry wanted to see the White House, so Mandell obliged by giving the boys a little tour before going to the

Arena. While they drove around, Harry said, "I forgot to ask who you're fighting." Harry looked at Cardione.

"Rocco Marcheggy, Rocky Marcheesi, Rocky somebody. Some Italian from Providence."

"He any good?"

"He comes to New York to train every once in a while, but at the downtown gyms. Golden Gloves. I hear he's knocked everybody out."

At the Arena, Mandell and Harry went with Cardione to his dressing room. They stayed with him and talked a little fight strategy. His bout was the opener on the card. Harry took a look at the fight program. It listed Rocky Marciano at 179 pounds and Gilbert Cardione at 189 pounds. Mandell and Harry figured that Cardione was bigger; he should fight inside and do a lot of clinching.

Mandell, as Cardione's manager, was going to be in his corner, and he asked Harry to be with him. It was the first time Harry was inside a fighter's corner, and he stood right behind Mandell and the cut man for the opening bell.

Just seconds into the first round, Marciano hit Cardione with a shot so hard that Cardione appeared to fall dead to the floor. Cardione hit the canvas like lead, and the crowd gasped as he was carted out of the ring on a stretcher. Mandell and Harry followed into the dressing room. Cardione was still unconscious for many minutes as the ring doctors administered to him.

To everyone's relief, Cardione finally opened his eyes. After he came to, Mandell and Harry helped him dress. They were so relieved to see him awake that they skipped their plan to stay to see the rest of the card. Mandell brought the car around, and Harry helped Cardione out of the Arena. The three then went to a nearby restaurant to get something to eat. Cardione was looking better and did not appear to have any lingering effects from getting hit by the "Marciano" sledgehammer, but he was very quiet and barely ate any of the food on his plate.

After finishing at the restaurant, they returned to the car and began the long drive back to New York. Mandell had been instructed by the doctors not to let Cardione fall asleep on the ride, so Harry sat in the back as a precaution. Cardione was still extremely quiet as he sat staring out the window into the darkness.

The car entered the tunnel around Baltimore, and the glaring, bright lights of the tunnel shocked Cardione out of his stupor. He began to get agitated and animated. When the car returned to the darkness as they exited the tunnel, Cardione started blabbering nervously.

"Harry, Harry, it's dark out. How far is the Arena? Are we gonna make it on time? We're gonna miss the fight!"

"Gilbert," Harry said.

Cardione interrupted. "Harry, Harry we can't miss the fight."

"Easy, Gilbert," Harry said, "It's been more than four hours. Don't you remember?"

"The fight's over?"

"It's over."

Cardione just stared back, a blank expression on his face. He would not have known that he had been in a fight that night, except for the fifty dollars that Mandell slipped into his shirt pocket.

Career Bouts

BY OCTOBER 1948, Harry was back training at Stillman's gym. Soon he was battling against a series of opponents.

October 11, 1948

Harry Haft (4–0) v. Gilbert Cardione (0–2)
Eastern Parkway Arena, Brooklyn, New York
    Mandell got a two-way payday as the manager of both fighters. Harry knocked out Cardione again in round two.

October 19, 1948

Harry Haft (5–0) v. Angel Martinez (4–5)
Columbia Park, North Bergen, New Jersey
    Harry won a hard-fought six-round decision. He swarmed his opponent in the final round, battering Martinez and bringing the crowd to its feet.

December 2, 1948

Harry Haft (6–0) v. Patsy Ricardo (0–0)
Wilkes-Barre, Pennsylvania
    Harry scored an easy one-round knockout.

December 8, 1948

(7–0) v. Jimmy Richards (21–5–1)

Binghamton, New York

Harry won a narrow decision over the experienced Jimmy Richards.

December 16, 1948

Harry Haft (8–0) v. Don Jabbora (4–0)

Paterson Armory, Paterson, New Jersey

This battle of the hitherto undefeated ended with Harry earning a close decision.

December 20, 1948

Harry Haft (9–0) v. Don Jabbora (4–1)

Paterson Armory, Paterson, New Jersey

This rematch was the under card of a Joe Louis v. Pat Comiskey main event. Harry earned another decision over Jabbora. Harry was now 10–0. He was ready for a main event.

January 5, 1949

Harry Haft (10–0) v. Pat O'Connor (10–10–3)

County Center, White Plains, New York

There was a huge crowd the night of the fight between Harry Haft and Pat O'Connor. White Plains had a large Irish immigrant population. They were out in droves to cheer on their hometown boy, and plenty a pint had been guzzled by the time the fighters entered the ring for the feature match.

O'Connor entered the ring to deafening cheers. Harry was in the ring already, bobbing and weaving to warm up. O'Connor gestured to the crowd, some of whom were waving the Irish flag, took off his championship belt, and tossed it to one of his handlers.

Because it was a middleweight bout, Harry would have to lose eight or nine pounds in just a couple of days, so he ran and sweated to make the weight.

"You know the belt is bullshit," Mandell told Harry.

Mandell was right. Although O'Connor was advertised as the "Middleweight Champ of Ireland," the real truth was that O'Connor was 4–10 in the United Kingdom. In his only match in Ireland, he had been knocked out in the first round.

Harry was not intimidated, not by the belt or by the raucous crowd. Harry even tried to forget the quote in the local paper that picked "O'Connor to win without using his shillelagh."

The fighters were introduced, instructions were given by the referee, and then the bell rang to start the fight.

Harry was taken by surprise. O'Connor was a southpaw. Harry had never fought a left-handed fighter before, or trained with one. To make matters worse, O'Connor was lighter and faster, making him difficult to hit. When Harry was able to land a punch, O'Connor clinched, and a head butt in the second round opened a gash under Harry's right eye. The cut became O'Connor's target for the rest of the fight, and he rubbed at it with his gloves in clinches as well as continuing to butt his head into it.

Harry fought through the blood for eight rounds. The judges gave the decision to O'Connor. Harry was angry with Mandell

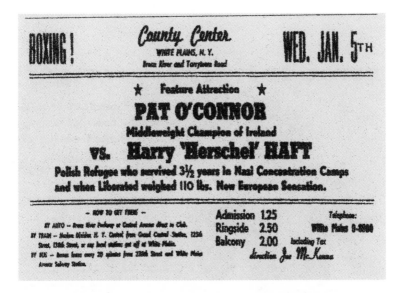

Flyer distributed for the Pat O'Connor fight. Courtesy of the author.

after the loss, feeling that his manager should have known that O'Connor was a southpaw to prepare him better.

This fight was Harry's first loss.

February 3, 1949

Harry Haft (10–1) V. Dom Bernardo (9–0)

Rochester, New York

Haft and Bernardo slammed each other in every round. Both fighters were decked in the second, and both staged rallies and counter-rallies. Here was a street fight, with no finesse boxing demonstrated. The crowd howled with appreciation from the opening bell. Both fighters were bleeding from the eyes and the ring canvas was spattered with blood. Referee Joey Emanuel

Who is Harry (Herschell) Haft?

Read What Leonard Cohen Prominent Sports Writer for NY Post Home News Wrote About Him Recently

During the war years Harry Herschell Haft was fighting in concentration camps for the extra ration of bread he received for entertaining prison camp guards. Now he is dwelling in Paterson, N.J., with an aunt and uncle and making his living as a professional boxer.

His relatives, who brought him here after the war, frown upon his ring career. His aunt said, "Didn't you undergo enough punishment?"

But the 24-year-old Haft replied, "After all I've been through, what harm can a man with gloves on his hands do me?"

He's been through plenty.

Placed in one concentration camp after another since he was 16, Harry has been shot, bayonetted and lashed by Nazi guards. He toiled for 18 months in a coal mine. Barely existing on the starvation diet he was allowed, he weighed but 110 pounds when he was finally liberated by the 150th Engineers. He remembers particularly the kind treatment he received from a medical Capt. Picos and from the 13th Infantry, a Negro division.

"Please tell your readers that I and thousands of other war victims are alive today because of sports. In Palestine today, despite the fighting, the Jewish people are sports fans and competitors. Your drive for sports equipment for the kids in the DP camps is a fine idea.

Gnarled Fingers Souvenirs of Fights to Finish

"As a boy in Lutz, Austria, I boxed with others in my neighborhood. When the Nazi guards called for boxers, soccer players, musicians, to entertain them, I went in for boxing because it meant I would get extra bread.

"Those were tough fights. We used ordinary winter gloves, no boxing gloves, and sometimes we fought with bare fists. No fight was over till one man was completely unconscious. Look at my hands," he said.

There were broken, misshapen knuckles on each hand. Three fingers on his left hand were not very pretty to look at. "One of my brothers escaped from a camp. They put my hand in a door and tried to get me to talk," he said simply, without any effort at heroics.

He has a bullet wound in his back. He also has a life-time souvenir from bayonet and pitchfork marks on his back incurred when Nazi guards were hunting for him in a stack of straw.

Let's skip the grisly details of his wartime experiences. He returned to Munich after hostilities ended. There in 1947 he won both the amateur heavyweight and light-heavyweight championships staged for U. S. troops and received cups from Gen. Lucius Clay.

So when he came to America, Haft felt the ring offered him his best chance to earn some money. He and a sister still abroad are the survivors of a family that included six other children. "I feel my mother would want me to fight in the ring, and I convinced my aunt and uncle here of that," he explained.

Since Cohen wrote the above article Haft has taken part in 5 additional bouts in New York and his complete record shows that he won 14 of the 15 contests he engaged in since coming to this country.

Most everyone enjoys watching a good fight so whether you are of Jewish extraction or Gentile (an a Heathen) why not make your plans to come to the Main and Beaver Streets Arena and see that fighter in action. His opponent is Toby Reid one of the best 160 pounders around these parts, won 17 of his last 18 bouts. See these two terrific punchers in action. Five other action filled bouts will also be presented for your enjoyment.

REMEMBER THERE ARE 6 FIGHTS EVERY TUESDAY NIGHT AT THE
ARENA Main & Beaver Streets 8:30 P.M.
Jimmie Murdock, Promoter

Gen. Adm. 1.00 & 1.25   Ringside 1.50 &

All of the above prices include Gov. Tax.

Flyer promoting Harry Haft. Courtesy of the author.

stopped the fight at 2:08 of the fifth round, with Harry on his haunches, trying to get up to resume battle.

For the first time, Harry was knocked out. Although they were offered a rematch, Harry's manager decided to head to Florida.

February 8, 1949

Harry Haft (10–2) v. Toby Reid (0–0)
Main and Beaver St. Arena, Jacksonville, Florida

Jacksonville promoter Jimmy Murdock shamelessly hyped this fight as a battle between Christians and Jews. He advertised Harry's record as 14–1 and Toby Reid's record as 17–1, all made up for publicity.

Harry sent Reid to the canvas three times and had him bleeding from ear to ear for seven rounds when beer bottles and other missiles start flying into the ring. Referee Natie Brown disqualified Harry for head butting in order to quiet the angry mob.

March 28, 1949

Harry Haft (10–3) v. Henry Chemel (55–24–1)
Causeway Arena, Miami Beach, Florida

Harry sweated off ten pounds on fight day to make weight for this middleweight bout. Worn down by veteran Chemel, Harry was knocked out in round nine.

• • •

After the loss to Chemel, Harry's fourth in a row, Mandell abandoned Harry in Miami Beach, skipping out on outstanding bills.

If Not Delivered
Return to—
RINGSIDE SPORTS WEEKLY
P. O. Box 2714, Miami 17, Fla.
Return Postage Guaranteed

International Ironmen Slug It Out Monday

Jewish light heavyweight Harry Herschell Haft makes his Miami debut at the Causeway arena, Monday night in a 10 round match with Henry Chemel, the Portland Pole.

Haft from all reports is one of those individuals who is a throwback to that ilk of ringmen who knew not otherwise than to start throwing punches when the opening gong rings, and has to be shunted aside by the referee, at the clang of the final bell. His experience of fighting for his life in the concentration camps of Europe, have given him an attitude that nothing that happens in the hempen square can be more severe than some past suffered brutality. Harry's standard answer is "After all I've been through, what harm can a man with gloves on his hands do me?"

Haft has been shot, bayonetted, beaten by pitchforks and lashed by Nazi guards. He stood 18 months of labor in a coal mine on a starvation diet, and weighed 110 pounds when rescued by American troops. On his release he was returned to Munich where in 1947, he won the amateur light heavy and heavyweight titles in tournaments staged for U. S. troops, and received cups from Gen. Lucius Clay.

Haft came to America, and decided

THE RINGSIDE SPORTS WEEKLY

P. O. Box 2714, Miami, Fla.
Published Every Friday

JACK DORAN
Editor and Publisher
HARRY SPEAR
Circulation Manager

WALTER STEVENS

Walter Stevens, Miami (via Newark, N. J.) lightweight. Stevens has his work cut out for him when he meets capable Snooks Howard in the eight round semi-final at the Causeway arena, Monday.

on a boxing career, first selling his aunt and uncle with whom he resides on the idea. His initial New York appearance resulted in a two round kayo, and the record shows nine straight wins compiled between August, and December. In eight succeeding contests he has an overall record of 16 wins, and two losses. Harry took Jacksonville fans by storm on March 8, when he battled Toby Reid, but suffered a disqualification in the seventh round, after sending Reid to the canvas three times.

Haft's desire to win and favorably impress Miami's followers of fistiana, assures a battle of terrific savagery.

Chemel, needs no introduction anywhere in the nation. Henry has been battling the leaders for a decade. His only severe local setback was when a badly cut mouth sustain in the opening round of his fight with Jimmy Curl, caused a cessation of hostilities. He is a spoiler and a trial

horse par excellence. There is no move in the manly art that he hasn't learned by virtue of his natural ability, and long experience between the ropes.

Possessing the sturdiness of an oak, heart of a lion, tenacity of a terrier, and the durability of old man river, Chemel can be counted on to extend the Jewish aspirant to the limit. He is all fighter. The fans should witness a contest between this pair, as though they were fighting for the ashes of their fathers, and the temples of their gods, before the conqueror emerges victorious.

Promoter Dave White, has completed an attractive set of bouts to complete the card. Lightweights Snooks Howard, and Walter Stevens, formerly of Newark. N. J., hookup in the eight round semi-final, that figures to be a fast hard fought scrap.

Stevens a recent arrival intends to stay in Miami, having brought his wife and family and established a home here. A rangy fine looking athlete he made his debut by taking a decision over the hard to beat southpaw Ernest Noques. Due to a layoff and the fact that the portsiders are a general nuisance Stevens was at a disadvantage in that match. Howard is the most consistent and pleasing of the local semi finalists. Snooks also took the honors in his last start, winning over Tony La-Rocco last Wednesday.

Larry Ray, Detroiter, who dropped a duke to Billy Moore, tackles veteran Jack Larrimore in a special six rounder. Jack is hitting the comeback trail with a vengeance and is in top form.

The Hill brothers, reputed to be as rugged as the hills of their native New England make their bow in the two remaining bouts. Billy Hill, will try to overcome popular Billy Spangler, in a sixer, and Paul Hill will be out to take the measure of Lefty Torres, Havana entry, in the opening four.

Boxing newsletter featuring Harry Haft's fight against Henry Chemel. Courtesy of the author.

Harry didn't know anyone who could help him get home, so he telephoned Stillman's and spoke to a boxer friend named Georgie Kaplan. Harry remembered that Georgie had an uncle in Miami, who he hoped might lend him some money to get home. Kaplan gave Harry his uncle's name and phone number.

The uncle's name was Meyer Lansky. Harry called him, introduced himself as a friend of Georgie, and explained his predicament. Lansky agreed to meet Harry in a small restaurant near the Miami Kennel Club at the tip of Miami Beach.

"So, you know my nephew Georgie?" Lansky asked him and invited him to sit down.

"We're friends."

"I called Georgie after we spoke and he vouched for you. He told me about you, the camps. I can see the numbers on your arm."

"My manager left me here in Miami and I have no means of getting back to New York. Georgie told me that you could loan me some money."

"I have no problem giving you a loan so long as it's to get you home, not for broads, or betting on the dogs," and he pointed in the direction of the track down the street.

"You're a nice-looking boy. I don't think you got any problems with the girls. Am I right?"

Harry grinned, and Lansky talked on.

"Georgie could be a great fighter, but he cannot get his mind off the girls. Been to his massage parlor on 8th Avenue?"

Harry shook his head no, and Lansky continued.

"You know, if Georgie would have a heart to fight like I have brains for business, I could have made him a champ."

Lansky reached into his pocket and pulled out a roll of money. He peeled off five twenty-dollar bills and handed them to Harry. Harry thanked him, and it was apparent the visit was over.

"A hundred bucks won't make up for those Nazi bastards— but it's yours. It's not a loan. There's no payback. *Zay gezundt* [bless you]."

Harry bought a one-way train ticket to Jacksonville.

April 12, 1949

Harry Haft (10–4) v. Danny Ruggerio (6–17–1)
Jacksonville, Florida

Harry, without a manager, went ten rounds and lost a decision. He now had enough money to go home.

May 30, 1949

Harry Haft (10–5) v. Johnny Pretzie (7–8)
Coney Island Velodrome, Brooklyn, New York

Harry reconciled with Mandell for this comeback fight. Harry punished Pretzie, at 191 pounds, for four rounds, with referee Ray Miller stopping the bout at 2:25 of the fourth round. Harry impressed Coney Island promoters, and Mandell promised to get Harry back in the ring.

The promoters at Coney Island liked the action that Harry brought. They gave him a shot at the feature event a month later. Harry was prepared to meet Gino Buonovino, but because of illness, he backed out. Mandell and Harry were told that Roland LaStarza would be the substitute fighter.

June 27, 1949

Harry Haft (11–5) v. Roland LaStarza (32–0)
Coney Island Velodrome, Brooklyn, New York

Roland LaStarza was a world-class fighter with a 32–0 record. LaStarza had already kayoed Buonovino in February, and Mandell was not sure Harry was ready for him.

There was great temptation to fight LaStarza to capitalize on his publicity, not to mention the fact that Madison Square Garden promoter Harry Markson would no doubt be present for this match.

Harry was not afraid of LaStarza or his big reputation. He had sparred with LaStarza dozens of rounds at Stillman's. LaStarza had never hurt Harry in the gym, and he felt sure this was a great opportunity. He knew LaStarza's style of hit and run rather than straight punching, and Harry thought at 172 pounds to LaStarza's 185, he had a shot to beat him.

The first three rounds saw Harry chasing LaStarza all over the ring, trying to land a knockout blow. Early in round four, Harry threw a wild right, and LaStarza scored with a combination to his jaw. According to Harry, he then slipped on a spot of sweat and fell to the canvas.

Referee Teddy Martin could barely voice a one count before Harry immediately rose and steadied himself by grabbing the rope with his right hand, and dropping his left. Mandell screamed at Harry to go to his knee to take the mandatory eight count, but

Harry was shaken up and thinking "European rules," where the eight count is taken standing. Harry made a big mistake. Referee Martin jumped in to separate the men and stopped the fight. Harry screamed, "Why are you stopping?"

Mandell went crazy in the corner. He erupted in a noisy protest to Chief Deputy Commissioner Dan Dowd and Deputy Commissioner Pat Callahan in the front row, but all in vain. Teddy Martin tried to calm Harry down.

"I told you to defend yourself at all times," he told Harry.

Harry was sick about the loss. It was an opportunity to revive his dream of fame by defeating an undefeated fighter, and he made a bonehead mistake. Dan Parker, columnist for the *New York Daily Mirror*, dismissed his excuse. "Shame on Harry (Hershel) Haft," he wrote. "Haft has been in this country long enough to know how to fight by American rules."

Harry had no one who wanted to listen to his lame excuse. Harry spent the next few days alone in Brighton Beach, depressed, without a job, and worried about his future. Then the telephone rang.

"Harry. Get back in training," said Mandell.

"What's doing?"

"I got you a fight that can get us back in the game."

"Against who?"

"Rocky Marciano," Mandell answered.

"When?"

"July 18 in Providence."

"I'll be at Stillman's in the morning."

"See ya there."

Training for Marciano

MANDELL MET HARRY at Stillman's about 11:00 the next morning. Accompanying Mandell was Saul Chernoff, a Paterson businessman and Mandell's new partner. Chernoff had bought a piece of Harry's contract that would allow them to go up to Greenwood Lake for eight or nine days of training. Here was some good news, since Greenwood Lake was the finest training facility in the area. At Greenwood Lake, Harry could leave behind all the distractions of the city and concentrate on the Marciano fight, which he knew would be his last shot. His careers, his dreams, his hopes of finding Leah through his celebrity were all on the line. He needed to win, and he had so little time to prepare.

Chernoff and Mandell picked up Harry in Brighton Beach on Saturday, July 9, and drove up to Brown's Hotel at the Lake. All three shared one room, with an open account for food and the use of the facilities. The togetherness was designed to keep Harry focused, and except for the nights that Chernoff and Mandell went off to the trotters or took in a show at one of the Catskill hotels, they all ate, drank, breathed, and slept the Marciano fight.

Harry trained like he had never trained before. At 6:00 every morning, Harry ran ten miles through the peaceful country with Mandell and Chernoff following closely behind in the car. When

141

he returned to the training camp, Harry would eat a big breakfast in the dining room and then walk another five or six miles before going back to the room for a nap. At 2:00 P.M. Harry went to the gym, where he shadowboxed, jumped rope, and worked on the speed and heavy bags. There, on July 11, Harry ran into Charley Goldman. Harry knew Charley Goldman from Stillman's Gym, where Harry had sparred with one of Charley's fighters, Caesar Brion, a top heavyweight.

Goldman gave Harry a big smile when he saw him.

"We have another Polack in the gym," Goldman announced. He, too, was a Polish Jew.

"Hello, Charley."

Charley Goldman was a former top bantamweight from forty years earlier who had fought some two hundred battles. He was now a respected trainer who had already trained three world champions. He appeared gnomelike because of his five-one height and stocky build. He always wore a derby hat in honor of Terry McGovern, a derby-wearing featherweight champ from the turn of the century whom Goldman idolized as a youth.

For some reason, Charley got personal with Harry. "Ever tell you my real name?" he asked.

"No," Harry said.

"Israel," he whispered. "But don't ever call me that."

"No, never."

"Hitler got my relatives in Warsaw," Charley told Harry confidentially.

Harry Mandell came over and stuck his two cents in. "Aren't you training Marciano?"

"I am. I'm going up Wednesday to get him ready."

"How can you stomach that scumbag manager Al Weill?"

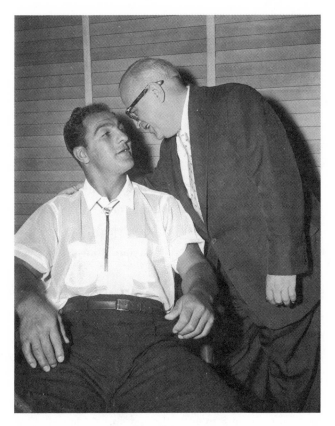

Rocky Marciano with Al Weill, his manager.
Courtesy of *The Ring*.

Charley was too much of a gentleman to take the bait, so he responded diplomatically, "As long as he lets me do my job, my way, we can get along."

Harry got bold and implored Goldman, "Charley, maybe you can help me?" He repeated the words in Yiddish, and he put his hand on Charley's arm.

Charley's eyes looked over to the tattoo on Harry's left forearm, and he read the green numbers out loud. "144738. Harry, you mean there were one hundred and forty-four thousand before you?"

"My lucky numbers," said Harry.

At that moment they looked in each other's eyes and felt a bond. Harry felt the same kinship toward Charley as a brother sharing that piece of bread in the camp to help each other survive.

"I have a couple of ideas for you, Harry," Charley said. "I want you to spar with Arturo Godoy. You know, he went the distance with Louis. He's older, smarter, and will get you used to being murdered inside." His hand brushed Harry's midsection. "Marciano hits hard. I'll be here today and tomorrow and I'll give you a look."

So, for the next two days, Charley Goldman prepared Harry to fight his own fighter. Then he left Greenwood Lake for Providence to train Rocky Marciano.

Mandell searched his brain for anything that could give Harry an edge. Greenwood Lake was near the Catskill Mountain resort area. One night, Mandell and his new partner went over to Grossingers to have a meal and see a show. Mandell was really trying to get to Monticello Raceway to do some gambling, but his partner wanted to see Arthur Ellen, the hypnotist, who had a popular nightly show where he made members of the audience entertain by singing or dancing or performing feats of strength while under his trance.

Mandell was mesmerized by the show, and he did not want to leave even to go bet on the horses, especially when Ellen started commanding his subjects to act. He made them laugh or cry at will, eat imaginary ice cream, assume new identities, and such things. But the most interesting part of the show involved posthypnotic suggestions. Ellen put people in trances, gave them specific instructions, and then brought them out of the trance. Later during the show, that subject would hear a bell ring and act on Ellen's instructions—for instance, stand up at his table and shout, "Hooray for Captain Spalding."

The audience roared with laughter every time Ellen rang the large cowbell, and the subject repeated the same bit. That bell gave Mandell an idea. At the end of the show, he left his partner in the bar and went backstage to talk to Ellen. He cornered Ellen in his dressing room.

"Mr. Ellen, could hypnotism be used to help a boxer win an important fight?"

"Of course," Ellen answered. "But only in the hands of an expertly trained hypnotist."

"Well, what I'm getting at is I've got a fighter over at Greenwood Lake who has lost a few fights in a row and needs to beat an unbeaten boxer. Can you help?"

Ellen nodded yes. "Hypnotism can bring out the best in all athletes by resolving all the causes of those inhibitions that are responsible for keeping them from performing at their very best."

Mandell's sales pitch was simple. If Ellen hypnotized Harry, without a fee, and Harry beat Marciano, Mandell promised to give Ellen all the credit and publicity.

Ellen was very interested. He was already envisioning a bigger career for himself hypnotizing athletes and other celebrities. He cautioned Mandell that he could not work miracles, but if his fighter had the talent, and was susceptible to hypnosis, he could free him of all distractions and help him realize his full potential. (Ten years later, Arthur Ellen had his own office in a medical building on Wilshire Boulevard in Los Angeles, where he worked with golfers Tony Lima and Ken Venturi, baseball players Maury Wills, Richie Allen, and Orlando Cepeda, and actors Tony Curtis, Fernando Lamas, and Liberace, among others.)

Ellen agreed, and arrangements were made to meet Harry at Greenwood Lake two days before the fight. Mandell and Ellen shook hands, and Mandell returned to the lounge to find Chernoff and share his news.

On Saturday, July 16, 1949, Ellen arrived at Greenwood Lake just after 11:00 A.M. He came into the gym to meet Mandell. Harry had just finished working on the speed bag and was jumping rope. Mandell brought Ellen over to introduce him.

Harry stopped jumping, caught a breath and extended a sweaty hand.

"Feeling like a champ?" Ellen asked, "Are you ready for the fight?"

"Did my manager tell you? All the pressure's on this one. Everything I worked for depends on this fight."

"Does that make you nervous, son?"

"What do you think?" Harry asked.

"Tell me Harry. What are some of your biggest concerns about the fight?"

"Ever see Marciano fight? I have. He can hit."

"Are you afraid?"

"You cannot be afraid."

"What else about the fight have you been thinking about?"

"Well, see my eyes, they can get cut. I've had stitches. If I bleed, I'm in trouble."

"Anything else?"

"It's just that I gotta win."

Ellen asked Mandell if there was a quiet room that they could go to, and Mandell cleared out a large broom closet and brought in two chairs. Ellen went into the room alone with Harry and faced the chairs several feet apart. They both sat down, and Ellen took out two candles from his pocket, lighted them, put them on the floor, and shut off the overhead light.

He told Harry in a quiet rhythmic tone to relax, and Harry was able to do that. He told Harry that his eyelids and arms were heavy, and within seconds, Harry was in a trance. Harry listened with eyes closed as Ellen intoned over and over, "You are not afraid of Marciano. Marciano will not hurt you. You will not feel his punches. Your eyes will not bleed. You are not afraid of Marciano. Marciano will not hurt you. You will not feel his punches. Your eyes will not bleed."

Over and over, Ellen put those thoughts into Harry's subconscious. Minutes later, Ellen told Harry that he would count to ten, whereupon Harry would open his eyes and not remember anything until he heard the ring of the bell to start the Marciano fight.

Ellen counted slowly to ten.

Harry opened his eyes.

"I feel rested." Harry said.

"Good." Said Ellen, "You are ready for the fight."

Fighting Rocky

HARRY, CHERNOFF, AND MANDELL drove to Providence that Sunday afternoon and checked into a nice downtown hotel, just a few blocks from the Auditorium.

The morning of the fight Harry rested until just after 11:00 a.m. He was hungry and thought he would get a light lunch at a sandwich shop near the hotel. As he walked through the hotel lobby he ran into Maxie Rosenbloom, a former light heavyweight champion who was now known more for his comedy act than his boxing record. In show business, he was known as Slapsie Maxie Rosenbloom, and he recognized Harry as he was making his way through the lobby.

"Hey, Harry, How are ya?" Maxie called out.

Everyone knew Maxie. He was a fixture around the gyms.

"Maxie, what are you doing here?"

"I'm reporting on the fight."

Maxie showed Harry his press credentials. Harry never knew when to take Maxie seriously.

"So, you're a reporter, huh?"

"Sure."

"No kidding?"

"No kidding," assured Maxie. "As a matter of fact, I'm

going over to see Al and Marty Weill and get an interview with Rocky."

"I'm the one you should be doing a story on."

"Why? You got no chance."

"Look, this fight is important to me. I'm in good shape and I've never trained harder. I'm going to be the first to knock Marciano out."

"Oh yeah?"

"Plus, I'll let you in on a secret, Maxie. Charley Goldman has been working with me, and he thinks I can beat him."

"That I don't believe. Wanna make a bet on the fight? I'll give you ten to one."

Harry went for his pocket immediately, and pulled out two ten-dollar bills. "All I got is twenty."

"Okay," Maxie grabbed the money.

"But I want to bet you fifty," said Harry.

"Fifty? I'll take the action; I know you're good for it."

"It's me who'll be looking for you after the fight to collect," said Harry. "Hope you got five hundred dollars on you."

Harry and Maxie kibitzed for a few more moments, the way fighters play with each other. They put up their dukes, bobbed and weaved, and tried to slap each other in the face.

"I gotta go now and see the winners," teased Maxie. "You're in for quite a beating."

"Ah, to hell with you. You don't know what you're talking about. Make sure you don't disappear with my money."

Harry returned to his room. He had just handed Maxie all of the money in his pocket and now lunch was no longer on his agenda. He lay down on the bed, and before he knew it, it was 5:30 and Mandell knocked on the door.

Harry let him in.

"I'm hungry," Harry said. "I need to eat something before the fight."

"We'll stop for some steaks on the way in," replied Mandell. "After all, it's on Chernoff."

Twenty minutes later they were out the door and on the way to a small restaurant about a half a mile from the Arena. Mandell ordered a hamburger, and Harry had a small steak. Chernoff had some clam chowder and fried clams. After they finished their meal, Mandell suggested to Harry that they walk off the food. Chernoff took the car, and let Mandell and Harry walk the half mile to the Auditorium. Before they parted, Chernoff wished them luck and told them he'd be watching from a ringside seat near their corner.

Harry and his manager arrived at the Auditorium at 7:30 p.m. The fight was expected to go on about 9:30. Harry allowed himself to daydream a little as he dressed. Harry stared at the Star of David on his purple trunks before he slipped them on. It reminded him of all of his struggles in the concentration camps. He believed that this fight was also a fight for survival. He sat on the massage table, shirtless and shoeless, focusing on what he had to do.

The cut man came in and loosened him up, stretching his limbs and rubbing him down.

A little after eight, Charley Goldman walked in the dressing room.

"Harry," he said.

"What are you doing in here?" asked Harry, "It's good to see you, but I'm thinking you're in there with Marciano."

Charley shook his head, rolled his eyes and threw one hand in the air:

"Al and his brother Marty; one is bad enough, but both of them together. . . . What the hell did you say to Maxie Rosenbloom?"

"What do you mean?"

"What did you say?"

"I made him a bet."

"What else did ya say?"

"Fifty dollars at ten to one."

Charley was not getting the answer he wanted.

"You didn't tell him that I thought you could beat Rocky, did you?"

"What if I did?"

"Well, that's what Maxie told Marty and Al, and they tore into my ass."

"Shit. I didn't mean to get you in trouble. Maxie was telling me how I was gonna get my brains beat out, and I ran my mouth."

"Because of your mouth, I had to explain that I worked with you over at Greenwood Lake. When Al heard that, he blew up and started cursing me. Marty accused me of being a traitor."

Goldman fixed his glasses and looked right at Harry.

"When they were done with their yelling and screaming, I told them that for this fight I'm in no one's corner. I'm just gonna watch. So don't embarrass me out there."

"I'm going to fight my heart out."

"Then good luck," said Charley, "And remember what we worked on in the gym? He can murder you inside, so keep your distance." He left.

Harry sat on the edge of the table and waited. Mandell threw him a pair of socks and helped Harry lace up his black shoes.

Mandell went back to his seat in front of the table on a wood folding chair. Harry and his manager began to talk fight strategy and they were interrupted about when three strange men entered the dressing room.

For fifteen minutes, the men threatened to kill Harry if he won the fight. They insisted he go down in round one.

When the men left, Harry asked his manager what he should do.

Mandell shrugged his shoulders and said he didn't know what to do.

Harry lay back down on the massage table and closed his eyes.

Mandell paced the room and overheard Harry say, "Not here in America. Not over a prizefight."

The cut man knocked on the door and said it was time to go. Mandell slipped the eight ounces of leather over Harry's taped hands and tied them tightly. Harry pounded his fists together to try them out.

"Hershel, should we call a cop?"

"What are they gonna do for me back in Brooklyn?"

Mandell helped Harry put on his white robe, and together they walked through the door and down the hallway toward the ring. They were both rattled by the threats, but Harry alone carried the burden into the ring.

A slim gathering of 1,655 sat in the auditorium to watch the fight. As Harry walked toward the ring, his eyes scanned the seats looking for the men. He did not see any of them.

Marciano and a small entourage entered the ring to a mild chorus of cheers. The announcer introduced some local celebrities to the crowd and then it was time for the fight.

The fighters came to the center of the ring for instructions. This first opportunity for the two men to make eye contact and get a psychological edge went for naught. Harry's eyes were still looking into the seats for the thugs. He could not shake the feeling of fear. It was the first time he felt such a fear in the ring. He remembered back to the time when his life was filled with threats, and he had visions of dead bodies being tossed into the fires.

He went back to his corner to await the start of the fight. When the bell rang, Arthur Ellen's hypnotic trance overcame Harry's subconscious, and Harry came out fighting.

John Hanlon, a sports writer, was at the fight and recorded this account for the *Providence Journal*:

Marciano weighed in at 184 & $\frac{1}{2}$ to Haft's 174. Both fighters started carefully. Haft a rusher with very little style landed the first good punch in the first, a hard right to Marciano's stomach. Marciano in return tested his range with a long right to the jaw and that was that for the frame.

In the second, Marciano whose fanciers delight in describing as the man who lowers the boom began getting Haft ready for delivery, though the latter traded punch for punch in the first minute. Then, after that exchange, Marciano caught Haft with a long right to the jaw that sent the later reeling to the ropes. Rocky followed with two lefts to the head and had his man groggy at the bell.

Two hard punches to Haft's head—a left and a right—were Marciano's openers in the third. At the halfway mark, Haft rallied briefly. But it was too late. After several damaging blows to Haft's head, Rocky delivered the crushers. The first was a left coming up to the midsection. Then, as Haft doubled up from the force of the wallop, Marciano shot a short right—down and across to put Haft out of action.

Haft received a fine reception as he left the ring, for the spectators realized that he had made a game attempt against forbidding odds. Not once did he back away from Marciano's punishing right hand and on several occasions stood toe to toe and slugged it out with his heavier opponent.

Harry went back to his dressing room after the fight. He was unhurt and depressed and looked at Mandell with a terrible sense of sadness. He knew his career was over, and he faced an uncertain future.

Charley Goldman came into the dressing room about fifteen minutes later. Harry was already in his street clothes.

"What happened, Harry?"

Harry looked down and said nothing.

"I couldn't believe it," continued Goldman, "you take all his shots and you go down in a clinch from a body blow?"

Harry could not look Goldman in the eyes. He was ashamed of what he had done.

"Harry, what happened?" Goldman asked again. "You were ready. I had Arturo pounding you plenty in the belly."

Harry looked up. He said, "You mean you didn't hear?"

Mandell piped in, "Charley, you know nothing?"

"About what?" Goldman pleaded.

At that moment, Harry stopped Mandell. Harry saw from the look on Goldman's face that he was genuinely disappointed. Harry knew Goldman didn't know anything, and he did not want to involve him.

He told Mandell, "If he doesn't know anything, then there's no sense talking about it."

Goldman, now at the end of his patience, threw up his hands and asked for the last time, "Know anything about what?"

"Vince Foster!" Mandell said, and Harry stopped him again.

The Sports Editor's Column—
End of a Turbulent Life

VINCE FOSTER'S death in an automobile crackup was more
shocking than surprising to his Omaha friends. He had lived
a turbulent life; seemed destined to die a violent death. He had
lived as he died—tragically and sensationally. . . . The moments
of sadness and disappointment outnumbered the periods of success
and happiness in Foster's short life—both inside and outside of the
boxing ring. . . . A broken home put him on his own at an early
age. He was in and out of many minor jams. Sometimes they were
major jams, and landed him in court. Tragedy struck his family
life a year after he was married. A baby died shortly after its
birth. . . . Within the ring, he had moments of success, but always
failure eventually broke the bubble. As an amateur he won the
Omaha Golden Gloves, but failed in the Chicago semifinals. As a pro,
he was on the doorway of fame after knocking out Tony Pellone last
January. But he was a dismal failure when he was knocked out
by Charlie Fusari in the first round in May. He never fought again.

* * *

VINCE called on us a week ago last Saturday. He made the
visit to tell us that he hadn't given up boxing, that he was going
back to Chicago to start working out under direction of Jack Hurley.
He said he was going to drive his young sisters back to Pipestone,
Minn., then be in Chicago "by Tuesday or Wednesday." . . . That
would have been last week. But he never did get back to Chicago.
We weren't at all surprised that he changed his mind again and
delayed his return to Chicago. Because he didn't talk like he
meant business when we last saw him. He said he wanted to keep
on boxing, but in the next breath he expressed doubt. . . . He wasn't
happy with his manager. He thought Jack Hurley had been doing
too much talking about his bad points, and was harming him rather
than helping him in many of the publicity stunts. He seemed to be
just what he had been for a long time—a confused young man who
didn't know what he wanted to do.

* * *

WE'LL always think that Vince Foster potentially was the finest
fighter ever to come out of Nebraska. He didn't quite reach
the heights achieved by Ace Hudkins, Morrie Schlaifer and Tommy
Grogan, but we'll always think he could have done so—if he had
made the most of his opportunities. . . . He had great natural ability.
He could knock a man out with either hand. He had a fighter's
heart. In his makeup was enough meanness to make him happy
trying to punch another man silly. . . . But he wasn't willing to
make the sacrifices necessary to boxing success. He refused to lock
the doors to other interests, and be just a boxer for a few years.
He wanted to be a fighter and a Bible student and a playboy all at
the same time. . . . In the memory of most sports fans, Vince Foster
will be marked down as a young man who wasted his chances.

Floyd Olds, Sports Editor.

Vince Foster obituary. Courtesy of the *Omaha World-Herald*.

Harry was now losing his temper and becoming irrational. "I'm through with fighting, Charley," Harry screamed at him. "Just get out of here."

Charley's eyes widened when Harry lost his temper. Without another word, he left the room. He did not leave angry, but disappointed in the Polish Jew he had befriended.

Mandell tried to console Harry. "I can get you another fight."

"Don't bother. I'm through."

Harry's boxing career ended that night. He would never fight again.

● ● ●

The next morning, the news broke about the death of Vince Foster, which had occurred hours before Harry's fight against Rocky Marciano.

Ever after, Harry would wonder how the men who threatened him knew about Vince Foster's death before it was reported in the news. He never believed the news report that Vince Foster's death was the result of an accident.

Moving On

WHEN HIS BOXING CAREER was over, Harry found work as a hat blocker in a Manhattan factory. The job paid well and he considered himself fortunate, but in October 1949, the owner of the factory suddenly died in an automobile accident, and Harry was out of work.

Unable to find another job, and running short of money, he had to move from Brighton Beach to a less expensive room in a section of Brooklyn called Brownsville. An aunt of a factory coworker, a widow named Mrs. Lipstein, rented him a room in her second-floor apartment.

One Saturday evening in mid October, Harry took in an early movie, and came back to his room around 9:30 P.M. Thinking that Mrs. Lipstein was already in her room, he locked the front door with the chain and went to bed.

The phone rang, and Harry answered.

Miriam Wofsoniker, a twenty-year-old girl living with her parents and younger brother in the apartment below, was on the phone.

"Hi, I'm Miriam from downstairs. Your apartment is locked with the chain, and Mrs. Lipstein can't get in. She is standing here and asked me to call you to let her in."

"Oh, I'm sorry. I'll open the door. I thought she was home," he answered clumsily.

"I'll send her upstairs."

"What are all those voices I hear? Are you having a party?

"I have some friends over," answered Miriam. "I'm sorry for bothering you."

Just before Miriam hung up the phone, Harry said, "Wait— I've been living here for weeks and I've been trying to meet you."

"You have?" Miriam answered with surprise.

"Yes. It may sound strange, but I first saw you washing windows and I took a liking to you."

Miriam laughed and said, "You did?"

"Yes. Would you go out with me tomorrow?"

Miriam hesitated for a moment, and then said yes. She knew Mrs. Lipstein had a new boarder living with her. She had caught a glimpse of Harry coming in and out of the building. She returned to her friends and Harry hung up the phone and let Mrs. Lipstein in.

It was Sunday afternoon, and Harry took Miriam by bus to visit his former landlady in Brighton Beach. Miriam thought this date was very odd, but went along. Mrs. Wolf was very kind to the young couple and they spent several hours visiting with her. For Harry, it was like bringing a girl back to meet his mother.

That evening Harry spontaneously took Miriam to the Iceland Supper Club. Although he was short of money, he wanted to impress her when he learned that she had never been to a nightclub.

Their friendship developed quickly. Harry picked Miriam up after work at her job on Fulton Street at the Cook's Union on Monday. He was there again Tuesday. And on Wednesday, when he met her at the end of the workday, he asked her to marry him. She said yes.

Miriam took Harry to meet her Aunt Eva and Uncle Shenky. She told them of their intention to marry, but asked them to keep it a secret from her parents. Harry introduced Miriam to his brother Peretz, who had just come from Germany with his wife Rushka and son Arthur. Harry also took Miriam to Paterson to meet his cousins and Uncle Samuel and Aunt Sadie.

On November 19, 1949, they married at the Kings County Courthouse. Miriam had to pay for the license, since Harry was now completely broke. Miriam broke the news to her parents that she was married, and Harry moved downstairs into their apartment. Miriam's parents insisted on a Jewish wedding, and the ceremony and reception was held on March 22, 1950.

Their first child, a boy named Alan, was born on November 17, 1950. For Harry, marriage and parenthood presented new struggles. For a young man growing up without a father, just a few years out of concentration camp, and without a livelihood, he tried the best that he could.

Finding Leah

IN SEPTEMBER 1963, my father surprised our family with a vacation in Florida. I was thirteen, my sister Helene nine, and my younger brother Marty just five years old.

My father and mother met right after the end of his boxing career. After taking a series of sales jobs, my father wound up in the fruit business, with a store on Rutland Road in Brooklyn. The store was open seven days a week and most holidays, so for my father to announce that our family was going on a trip was something out of the ordinary.

He told us we were all going to Miami, and that the five of us would travel by train to save money. The trip from New York to Miami by train would take twenty-four hours, and I was very excited because it would be the first time our family would vacation out of the New York area.

We traveled coach class, which meant we slept in our reclining seats, and we ate fruit and sandwiches from home for our meals. When the train finally made its way into Florida, the scenery became very interesting. It was the first time we had seen oranges and grapefruits growing on trees.

When we arrived in Miami, we took a taxi to the Marseilles Hotel on Miami Beach. The Marseilles was a large family beachfront hotel near Lincoln Road. It served two kosher meals a day in a fine dining room and provided entertainment for its guests every evening.

We checked into one large room with two double beds and a rollaway for the five of us. I looked out the window of our room, and I could see the tower on Lincoln Road that displayed the time and temperature. It was seventy-nine degrees and approaching 11:00 A.M., and we all were anxious to get outside into the sunshine.

As my mother began unpacking, my father went right to the night table between the beds, opened the drawer, and pulled out the local telephone books. There was one book for Miami, another for Miami Beach. He threw them both on the bed.

"Miriam," he yelled to my mother, "take the kids down to the pool. Alan, you stay here. I'm going to need your help."

My mother, brother, and sister dressed for the pool and left us alone in the room.

"Alan, listen to me. I'm looking for a woman I knew in Poland. I was told she lives in Miami and her last name is Lieberman. When I knew her she was called Leah Pablanski. That was before the war."

"What do you want me to do, Popsie?"

He handed me the Miami and Vicinity phone book. "Could you look up Lieberman for me?" he asked.

I opened the book to the L's.

"Dad, there are many, many listings with the last name Lieberman."

"Are there any with the first name Leah?" he asked.

"None. What do you want me to do?"

"Call all the Liebermans, one by one, and ask for Leah. When you find her, hand me the phone."

My father took off his shirt and pants and lay in his underwear on the next bed watching television while I dialed. After many calls without success, I reached the home of a Michael Lieberman. He didn't hang up like the others when I asked for Leah.

"Who are you?" he asked.

"Is Leah there?"

"I'm her husband. Who is this?"

"My name is Alan Haft. Hold on please. Just a moment. I have someone here who is trying to reach her," and I handed the phone to my father.

"Hello, I am looking for Leah Pablanski. That was her name when I knew her in Poland before the war."

"And who are you?"

"We grew up in the same town—Belchatow."

"I am Leah's husband. Can I help you?"

"Is she there?"

"Yes."

"Can she come to the phone?"

"She's not taking any calls."

"I've been looking for her for a lot of years. Can I please talk to her?"

"Look, I told you she cannot come to the phone right now."

"I came all the way from New York and I was hoping to see her."

"I don't think that's going to be possible."

My father began to get frustrated. He could not seem to get the husband to bring Leah to the phone. I did not understand why my father insisted on seeing this woman. What did this call have to do with our family vacation?

I was anxious to join my brother and sister down by the pool. Before my father hung up, he begged: "Look, I'm here with my kids, my whole family. We're staying at the Marseilles Hotel in Miami Beach, room 256. Could you just tell her that Hertzka called; that Hertzka from Belchatow would like to see her? Thank you."

My father looked unhappy. "Let's go find your mother at the pool. Come on," he said. He got up to go find his bathing trunks, while I slipped mine on.

We were about to leave the room when the phone rang. I answered it.

"Hertzka?" I quickly handed the phone to my father.

"Yes?"

"Hello, I am Michael Lieberman. Look, I don't know you, but I told Leah you called. She wants to see you."

"We grew up together. We were just kids before the war."

Michael interrupted.

"She hasn't wanted any visitors, but when I mentioned your name, she asked me to call you right back. You, she wants to see."

"When can I come?" my father asked.

"Would tomorrow afternoon be good?"

"Sure it would. I'll rent a car. Can I put my son back on the phone to get directions from you?"

My father told me to grab the hotel pad and a pen. He handed me the receiver, and Mr. Lieberman gave me the directions.

Finally, we were able to join my mother at the pool where we enjoyed the rest of the day.

The next day my father rented a car, and asked only me to accompany him. I would have preferred to stay at the hotel, but my father had a way of asking that would not allow me to refuse. We drove over a bridge to Miami, and followed the directions until we found a neighborhood lush with trees. We found the address and pulled into the driveway. I followed my father as he got out of the car and knocked on the front door.

A man answered the door. He was wearing dungarees and a white T-shirt and he wore large rimmed glasses.

"I'm Michael Lieberman. You're Hertzka?"

"Harry. This boy is my son Alan."

"Come in," he welcomed us.

He brought us to the living room area and we were seated on a large floral couch. There was a plate of fruit and candies on the coffee table in front of us.

A teenage girl asked us if she could get us a drink.

"This is our daughter, Sarah," said Michael. "My son David is sleeping over at a friend's house."

Sarah brought a pitcher of lemonade and some glasses. Her father sat across from us in an upright chair and she placed the drink on the coffee table between us. She filled the glasses and then sat down next to her father in a matching upright chair.

There was an awkward silence as my father and I reached for our glasses and began to drink the lemonade.

Michael leaned forward with his hands clasped. Sarah smiled at us politely, and then put her eyes down.

"Leah has cancer," Michael said, and he paused to swallow. "She has been very sick from the drugs and the radiation. The doctors don't give us much hope."

A chill went through the warm air. My father's mouth was wide open and without words as he returned the glass to the tabletop. I had a hard time looking at Sarah, although I wanted to, as she was very pretty.

"I'm sorry Michael. I had no idea she was sick," my father spoke.

"It's okay. We haven't told many people."

"Thank you for letting me come to your home. Now I understand our phone call."

"Leah has refused to see any of our friends, and even relatives." Michael continued. "She is embarrassed at how she looks. She was such a beautiful woman."

My father nodded, "I know. We were kids before the war. She was beautiful. I knew her father and most of her family. We lost contact when I went into the camps. I looked for her after the war, and I never stopped wondering whether she survived."

"How did you find us?"

"I got a phone call from the Society, you know, the survivors from Belchatow. I contacted them a long time ago for information. And just last month, after fifteen years, they called to say she might be living in Miami, with a married name of Lieberman."

Michael replied, "Maybe when we applied last year for the reparations from Germany. I remember we did get a call. But she was not able to follow up, she was sick at the time. So, when you called, I didn't put it together. But when I told Leah your name, she knew and made me call you right back. She wanted to see you."

Tears welled up in Michael's eyes, and Sarah got out of her chair to comfort him.

Michael regained his composure, and patted his daughter's hand as he rose.

"This day is a happy one for your mother. It's a beautiful day outside. Let's enjoy it."

I must have looked stricken, because Michael motioned to me and said, "Alan, eat some of those cookies. Sarah made them."

"Leah is upstairs. She is a little weak, and I will need to help her down. And Harry, you understand that with the treatments, she's not looking like herself."

Michael went up to get her. The time spent waiting for her to appear bristled with suspense. Then she appeared at the top of the stairs in a bathrobe. She clung to the railing on one side, while grasping Michael's arm with her other hand as she descended down the stairs. Leah was nearly bald except for small patches of dark hair irregularly scattered on her skull. Her face was bone thin, and she had the look of someone who had been starved.

Her husband walked her over to us and we rose. Leah and my father stood face to face crying. My father was the toughest man on earth. I had never seen him cry. He just stood there sobbing, and Sarah gave him a napkin from the table to wipe his eyes.

Michael introduced me.

"This big boy is Harry's son, Alan."

Leah looked me over, and I could not help thinking that she was shocked at how fat I was.

"We have a son David," said Leah. "He is visiting at a friend's house." Then she turned to my father and asked, "Does my Sarah remind you of me?"

My father gave Leah a big smile and shook his head yes.

"Michael," Leah said, "I would like to spend some time alone with Hertzka. Hertzka, there's a bench in our backyard where we can sit and talk. Come with me."

Michael pointed to the door that led out to the yard, and said, "That's a good idea. Getting some fresh air will be good for you. We'll be here."

My father took Leah's arm and walked with her out the back door. We all sat back down, and Michael and Sarah attempted to entertain me with small talk. They asked me about my school, my family, my home in Brooklyn, and my thoughts about Florida. And then Michael explained to me why Leah wanted to take my father out into the backyard.

"I'm sure Leah is showing your father the fruit trees. She is so proud of them," Michael said to me. "They are so full of fruit. We have grapefruits, oranges, tangerines, key limes, and mangos. They were planted more than ten years ago when we first moved in. Now we have so much fruit that we give most of it away."

After a while, the back door opened and we stopped talking as my father and Leah came back into the room. Leah spoke first. "Thank you for a wonderful visit. We caught up on many things." Leah and my father were both holding hands and smiling. She let go of my father's hand and walked over to her daughter. "I hope you have taken good care of our guest," and she looked over to me and smiled. Then she turned to Michael and said, "It is beautiful outside, but the fresh air has tired me a little. And I am ready to go back upstairs." She said something in Yiddish to my father that I didn't understand. Then she said goodbye to me.

Michael had Sarah help her mother back to her room.

My father watched intently as Sarah and Leah navigated the stairs.

Michael looked at my father and then walked over and embraced him." I'm glad you came," he said. "I can tell how much Leah enjoyed your visit. It meant so much to her. She told me all about you last night. She was so happy to learn that you had survived."

Michael began crying. Sarah was just coming down the stairs to rejoin us and rushed to her father.

"I'm sorry," Michael said to us, apologizing for his crying, "It has been so difficult . . ."

Tears welled up in my father's eyes again, and he drew a deep breath. He turned to me and said, "We can go." We said our good-byes and we left.

We hit traffic on U.S. 1 going back to the hotel on Miami Beach. Not a single word was spoken between us. I tried to turn on the radio to break the silence, but my father pushed my hand away and said, "No music right now. I'm not in the mood."

It was quiet again. After a few minutes, my father spoke.

"Alan, it was good you came today. Someday, I'll tell you everything, and someday maybe you will write the story of my hard life."

Afterword

THIS BOOK TELLS A TRUE STORY. In September 2003, my father sat down with me, and for the first time told me the details of his life. We tape-recorded for two days, with a follow-up of several months of detailed questioning. The brutality, violence, and heartbreak my father experienced was more than any son could bear to hear, but I listened with detachment, trying to capture all I could. It was difficult for him to share these experiences with me, and he told his story as though he were telling the story of someone else's life. Most of the dialogue in the book is a faithful rendition of what my father said to me directly. Some dialogue, although invented, seeks to capture what my father understood to have taken place. The names of several important characters are fictitious. Chicky, the gangster; Schneider, the German officer; the American soldiers; Chernoff, a financial backer; and Leah's last name were not specifically remembered by my father.

It was during my college years, 1970–73, that my father first asked me to write the story of his life. I was the first-born son, and my father felt it was my obligation, but I managed to avoid it for thirty years. I had my reasons.

My greatest reluctance in hearing my father tell the story was that it would explain some of his behavior that I did not want to excuse. He was prone to fits of rage, and I remember being beaten for my childish misbehavior—like the time I used the curse words I had learned from him and was thrown to the ground and kicked until my mother was able to intervene. Our dining room had a brown stain on the ceiling from a cup of coffee that he launched during an argument with my mother. The night he drank a full bottle of whiskey and went out of the house, telling us that he was going to kill his business partner, I slept with a bottle under my pillow to protect myself should he return to direct his violence toward me.

My father was not like the other fathers in the Brooklyn neighborhood where I grew up. He was a big brute of a man, with a quick and irrational temper. He often embarrassed me. He spoke broken English with a thick accent, and he could barely read or write. He wasn't the dad who helped with homework or threw and caught a baseball with you. His left forearm bore ugly green numbers that had been tattooed on. They were a visible reminder that he came from another country, where he experienced horrors that he would never talk about. His hands were big, and bulky, with misshapen fingers. His nails were always dirty. He could never escape the memories of his years in the concentration camps. He lived with nightmares his entire life, and he was always threatening to kill himself by some violent means whenever a personal or family crisis arose. He took pleasure when I begged him with my tears not to do it. His pleasure, my pain. It was not until I reached adulthood that I realized that he would never do it.

As a young boy, I was proud of my father's toughness. He was known in our neighborhood as Harry the Fighter, and he expected me to carry on the tough-guy image.

To all who asked him about his fight with Rocky Marciano, he would tell the same story.

"Rocky was a hard puncher?" someone would ask.

"I wouldn't know. I didn't get a chance. The fight was fixed," he would answer.

"Waddya mean?" they would press.

"I was threatened. I had to lay down," he would answer. Although he never wavered from that version of the events, I never believed him. I saw it as an excuse for why he peddled fruit from a pushcart and from stores in crime-ridden Brooklyn ghetto neighborhoods.

About his concentration camp experiences, my father was stone silent. What little I learned came from overhearing conversations he had with other adults. My mother explained his irrational behavior, his violence, his suicide threats, by making vague references to his "background." It was a "background" that I did not want to hear about. Life with him in the present was scary enough.

By today's standards, I was an abused child. As I grew older, married, and had my own children, I struggled to understand and love my father. Unlike my brother and sister, I managed compassion and tried to be a good and caring son. I often asked myself, "How would I have turned out if I had his experiences? What kind of husband and father would I be?"

The last time I saw my father was days after his eightieth birthday.

"Alan, I am going to jump out my window and kill myself," he was commenting on the pain he was experiencing from his disabilities and illnesses.

"Popsie," I said. "You have been threatening to kill yourself since I was a kid, and you are not dead yet."

He flew into a rage and attempted to strike me with his cane. He thought I wanted him to do it.

I have spent my entire adult life trying to get my father to love me. The writing of this book was my last attempt. After learning firsthand what my father had to endure, I understand why he was who he was. I love him. And I forgive him.

I would like to thank John Radzilowski, adjunct professor of history at the University of St. Thomas in St. Paul, Minnesota, and senior fellow of the PIAST Institute. Dr. Radzilowski's background information on the history of Poland was instrumental in my understanding of the times in which my father lived.

I am especially grateful to Mike Silver, historian for the New York Veteran Boxer's Association and curator of the critically acclaimed exhibit "Sting Like a Maccabee: The Golden Age of the American Jewish Boxer" presented by the National Museum of American Jewish History in Philadelphia from 2004 to 2005. Mr. Silver gave freely of his time in helping contextualize my father's place in the sport of boxing.

Lastly, this book would never have come to be without the hard work and encouragement of my wife, Gail. She is and always has been my dream-maker.